What people

Allegories of the

C000120062

It has often been said that it is easier to imagine the end of the world than the end of capitalism. Milo Sweedler's highly readable and continually engaging book focuses on several recent films responsive in widely different ways to this lament. From considerations of the end of the world by celestial body to the creative destruction of financial markets, in both senses of the phrase, Sweedler places six "cinematic expressions of popular discontent" in a rich historical, theoretical, and aesthetic context, and demonstrates that, even in the bleakest circumstances, the hope of creating a better world survives.

Jeff Kinkle, co-author of *Cartographies of the Absolute*

Contradicting the assumption that popular film inculcates the masses with reactionary ruling-class ideologies, Sweedler argues that the motion picture industry cannot sell its wares if it ignores the real-world struggles of its viewing audience. If those struggles have become anti-capitalistic, so be it: films will find ways—at times direct, at times coded—to reflect the widespread discontent with global capitalism's failure to deliver on its promises. *Allegories of the End of Capitalism* ventures beyond the typical ambit of Hollywood Left productions to provide astute readings of six films from around the globe that agitate for revolution.

Kirk Boyle, co-editor of *The Great Recession in Fiction, Film, and Television: Twenty-First-Century Bust Culture*

Allegories of the End of Capitalism

Six Films on the Revolutions
of Our Times

Allegories of the End of Capitalism

Six Films on the Revolutions of Our Times

Milo Sweedler

Winchester, UK
Washington, USA

JOHN HUNT PUBLISHING

First published by Zero Books, 2020
Zero Books is an imprint of John Hunt Publishing Ltd., No. 3 East St., Alresford,
Hampshire SO24 9EE, UK
office@jhpbooks.com
www.johnhuntpublishing.com
www.zero-books.net

For distributor details and how to order please visit the 'Ordering' section on our website.

Text copyright: Milo Sweedler 2018

ISBN: 978 1 78535 862 3
978 1 78535 863 0 (ebook)
Library of Congress Control Number: 2019930341

A CIP catalogue record for this book is available from the British Library.

Design: Stuart Davies

UK: Printed and bound by CPI Group (UK) Ltd, Croydon, CR0 4YY
US: Printed and bound by Thomson-Shore, 7300 West Joy Road, Dexter, MI 48130

We operate a distinctive and ethical publishing philosophy in
all areas of our business, from our global network of authors to
production and worldwide distribution.

Contents

Acknowledgments x

Introduction 1

Chapter 1 The End of the World of the End: *Melancholia* 11

Chapter 2 The Demise of Finance Capital: *Cosmopolis* 35

Chapter 3 The Rationality of Revolt: *Suffragette* 64

Chapter 4 The Insurrection to Come: *Django Unchained* 96

Chapter 5 Negations of the Negation: *Elysium*
 and *Snowpiercer* 132

Endnotes 166

Bibliography 186

Also by the author

The Dismembered Community: Bataille, Blanchot, Leiris, and the Remains of Laure ISBN 978-0-87413-052-2
Rumble and Crash: Crises of Capitalism in Contemporary Film ISBN 978-1-4384-7297-9

For Chuck Kleinhans (1942–2017) in respectful memory

Acknowledgments

Many people contributed to the development of this book. Abderrahman Beggar, Hugo De Marinis, Patricia Elliot, Colman Hogan, Marta Marín-Dòmine, Sharon Marquart, Charles Nuckolls, Herbert Pimlott, Marc Olivier Reid, Margaret Toye, Christopher Treadwell, Kathleen Vanesian, and Heidi Yeandle offered encouragement, constructive criticism, and helpful suggestions. Above all, I wish to thank my mother, Marilyn Zeitlin, for the innumerable corrections and suggestions for improvements she made in her multiple readings of the manuscript.

An early version of chapter 1 appeared under the title "The End of the World of the End: Lars von Trier's *Melancholia* and Political Theory" in *A Critical Approach to the Apocalypse*, edited by Alexandra Simon-López and Heidi Yeandle (Oxford: Inter-Disciplinary Press, 2013). I am grateful to the publisher for permission to reprint the piece in revised form.

Introduction

What unites the films examined in this book is not a particular national cinema, the cultural heritage of the filmmakers, a specific genre, or even the movies' manifest narrative content. The filmmakers come from six different countries on four continents. Two of the films are set in the past, two take place in the present, and two are set in the future. One of the directors is a woman; the other five are men. The movies include a European art film, a British period drama, a postmodern cowboy movie, an offbeat political drama, and two dystopian science-fiction films. What brings together this diverse array of films is their refraction of a common problem: each of them allegorizes disenchantment with the neoliberal world order and proposes a vision of the system's violent demise.

How the movies allegorize this disenchantment varies from film to film. Thus Lars von Trier's *Melancholia*, for example, released in November 2011, at the peak of the anti-capitalist Occupy Wall Street protest movement, spends 2 hours patiently detailing the private concerns and petty intrigues of a group of super-rich socialites and then proceeds to demolish their world by setting a massive rogue planet on a collision course with Earth. The movie presents in this way two very different visions of "the end of history." On the one hand, it gives audio-visual form to the world of triumphant neoliberalism that neoconservative political scientist Francis Fukuyama celebrated in his 1992 manifesto, *The End of History and the Last Man*. On the other hand, it offers a fantasy vision of that same world's cataclysmic demise.

David Cronenberg's *Cosmopolis* (2012), shot during the months preceding the Occupy protests of fall–winter 2011, also allegorizes the violent destruction of capitalism, in this case by narrating the demise of a cutthroat New York billionaire whiz kid who metaphorically represents finance capital as such. The unscrupulous tycoon's downfall is represented in multiple ways in the film. Anti-capitalist street protesters trash the billionaire's luxury limousine as it inches its way across town toward a barbershop. The protagonist's own physical appearance changes correlatively over the course of the film from that of an imposing business executive to that of a ragged street punk, who, by the end of the movie, has half a haircut, the remnants of a cream pie on his face, and a hole in his hand from a self-inflicted pistol wound. These changes of appearance function as visual analogues of the trader's financial ruin, which results from a high-stakes bet that the financier placed on the Chinese yuan. The speculator's demise culminates in his assassination by a former employee that the bloodless tycoon laid off prior to the film action. Each of these narrative and visual elements contributes to making Cronenberg's *Cosmopolis* (based on Don DeLillo's 2003 novel of the same title) a striking allegory of events that took place around the time of filming, with the noteworthy difference that, in Cronenberg's version of events (as in DeLillo's), the antipathetic financier gets his comeuppance.

Sarah Gavron's *Suffragette* (2015) and Quentin Tarantino's *Django Unchained* (2012) derive their political currency from a common premise. Each film examines a phenomenon that is now generally considered backward, brutal, or barbaric but which, in the past, was widely accepted as natural or inevitable. *Suffragette* transports the viewer to an era when women in Britain did not have the right to vote, while *Django* takes us to a period in US history when African Americans in the southern states had the legal status of personal property. The films show members of those subaltern groups rising in revolt against a system of oppression that denies them political rights (in Gavron's film) or a modicum of human rights (in *Django*). The explosive political potential of the films in the present lies in the implicit connections that the movies suggest between attitudes, practices, and policies that were once status quo but are now intolerable, and a current state of affairs that we should no longer tolerate.

The connection that *Suffragette* forges between sexual discrimination and economic exploitation leaps off the screen from the moment the movie begins. The opening scene of women working in sweatshop conditions as their male overseer looks down on them from a post situated above the factory floor sets up a film narrative that superimposes images of class oppression and class struggle onto the story of the Votes for Women campaign in Edwardian England. The overarching reading of the film developed in chapter 3 of this book stems from Gavron and screenwriter Abi Morgan's preliminary decision to center their story of the British suffragettes on a group of working-class women, as opposed to the more famous upper-class women in the movement. This strategic decision on the filmmakers' part enables the spectator to link imaginarily the social situation depicted on the screen with the conditions of millions of workers, predominantly women, who labor for pennies an hour in the self-regulated, unmonitored, and tax-exempt Export Processing Zones that have sprung up around the world. At the same time, it permits the viewer to perceive the suffragettes' massive street rallies, their marches on Parliament, and even the acts of vandalism and sabotage that they commit, as episodes in a political general strike. By taking us back to a time when feminists threw stones through windows and blew up letterboxes in order to press their cause, Gavron's film implicitly proposes a course of action to the expanding ranks of the disenfranchised of the world.

The cultural politics of *Django Unchained* are also apparent in the movie's opening shots, which show a pair of white slave traders on horseback driving half a dozen shackled African slaves through the desert. However, in contrast to *Suffragette*, which offers a revisionist history of the militant women's suffrage movement in Britain, Tarantino's film proposes less a rewriting of history per se than a playful engagement with cinema history. The movie conjures two distinct time periods. On the one hand, on the level of the narrative, it locates us in the antebellum South of the United States. On the other hand, by virtue of its generic borrowings from the spaghetti Westerns of the 1960s and Blaxploitation films from the early 1970s, it simultaneously situates us in the heady years of "the sixties." Although the movie is set in the mid-nineteenth century, it looks like a film from the 1960s. The film analysis proposed in chapter 4 draws upon writings by a key author from each of those historical periods in order to explore the relation of the film's two time periods to the current situation. Moving from Marx's writings on slavery to what he calls "the general law of capitalist accumulation" in *Capital* (1867), the chapter argues that slavery is not an aberration of the capitalist system but, on the contrary, that it represents the asymptotic horizon to which global capitalism has been moving ever closer in recent decades. The chapter ends with concluding thoughts on the solution that Frantz Fanon proposes, in *The Wretched of the Earth* (1961), to the problem of neo-slavery in colonial Africa: "To destroy the colonial world means nothing less than demolishing the colonist's sector, burying it deep within the earth or banishing it from the territory."[1] It is precisely such a solution to the problem of institutionalized slavery—an institution that was at one and the same time a codified form of racial discrimination and a legal system of economic exploitation—that Tarantino proposes at the end of *Django Unchained*.

The last chapter examines two dystopian sci-fi films that imagine what the world will look like if it continues on its current trajectory of ever-increasing wealth inequality. Neill Blomkamp's *Elysium* (2013) and Bong Joon-ho's *Snowpiercer* (2013) both communicate a vision of sharp class divisions in which the upper class lives in guarded enclaves cut off from the swarming multitude of the abject poor, and both movies envision members of the lower class rising up against the ruling elite. The two films explicitly present themselves as allegories of the class struggle. However, rather than envisioning the revolt coming from the ranks of an international working class, as Marx and Friedrich Engels predicted it would in *The Communist Manifesto* (1848), these two movies perceive it coming from the lowest stratum of society: the destitute and reviled lumpenproletariat. Marx and Engels had nothing but contempt for this "passively rotting mass thrown off by the lowest layers of the old society."[2] However, Marx's later writings enable us to cast this group in a different light. As Marx perceived in *Capital*, the more efficiently and optimally the capitalist system runs (according to its own internal logic), the more of these "excess" people it leaves in its wake. The system is arguably running more optimally in the early twenty-first century than it has during any previous period in the history of capitalism. As the number of people discarded by the system grows, the likelihood of an insurrection on the part of the teeming multitude of the menially employed, the precariously employed, the unemployed, and the structurally unemployable increases. The book's closing chapter explores the ways that Blomkamp's and Bong Joon-ho's films give vivid expression to that hypothetical scenario.

In sum, I argue, all the films under examination—whether they are set in the past, the present, or the future; whether they recount the story of a slave's revolt, the agitation of militant feminists, or a cyborg's assault on a futuristic gated community—respond either directly or indirectly to the contradictions of contemporary global capitalism. The films do not, for the most part, frontally represent those contradictions. Rather, they transcode their effects in film narratives taking place at times and places as diverse as the antebellum US South, early twentieth-century London, and the sprawling slums of a future Los Angeles.

The idea that mass cultural artifacts such as feature films

reflect the social climate in which they were produced is by no means original to this book. In the 1920s, German film theorist and cultural critic Siegfried Kracauer famously argued that "the position that an epoch occupies in the historical process can be determined more strikingly from an analysis of its inconspicuous surface-level expressions than from that epoch's judgments about itself."[3] Surveying a wide array of pop-culture objects and spectacles, the essays collected in *The Mass Ornament* show how such products of mass consumption as bestsellers, popular films, variety shows, and dance performances express Weimar Germany's cultural unconscious. In *From Caligari to Hitler: A Psychological History of the German Film* (1947), Kracauer narrows the field of inquiry to one of those means of expression, arguing that the cinema exceeds other popular media in its ability to reflect "those deep layers of collective mentality which extend more or less below the dimension of consciousness."[4] In Kracauer's estimation, the specific properties of the moving-image medium make it more inclusive, and therefore more revealing, than such products of industrial culture as paperbacks, magazines, radio broadcasts, advertisements, and "other sedimentary products of a people's cultural life." "Owing to diverse camera activities, cutting and many special devices," he writes, "films are able, and therefore obliged, to scan the whole visible world."[5] The argument pertains to sci-fi and fantasy films as well as to more realistic fare. In either case, the theorist maintains, whether it depicts "current reality or an imaginary universe," the motion picture presents the viewer with what Kracauer, citing philosopher Horace Kallen, calls "visible hieroglyphs."[6] The critic's job is therefore less to analyze the movie's manifest narrative content than it is to draw out the implications of motifs that appear in the field of the moving image. If, as Kracauer suggests, once again citing Kallen, a movie is "a drama with two levels, a sequence of symbolic actions with a 'manifest content' and a 'latent content,'" the vocation of the film critic is to discern the latter in the field of the former.[7] That is, in essence, what this book sets out to do.

The skeptical reader may object at this point that narrative cinema is an unlikely place to look for evidence of popular resistance to global capitalism. Unlike Kracauer's *Caligari* book, which discerns the social circumstances leading to Hitler's rise to power in the films of the Weimar Republic, the present study examines how a survey of feature films from the early 2010s transcodes popular discontent with the global reign of capital. Analyzing six movies released between 2011 and 2015, it explores how films of different genres, produced in different parts of the world and by very different filmmakers, visualize, express a longing for, or implicitly call for an end to capital's unbridled reign. Surely the approach is misguided, the unsympathetic reader will protest. Doesn't the author see the incongruity between his object of study and his overarching thesis? The mass commodities produced by film studios—capitalist corporations at the heart of the culture industry—are not the first place one might think to look for expressions of popular discontent with global capitalism.

Kracauer addresses this apparent paradox in the introduction to his *Caligari* book. Although it is true, the author recognizes, that film studios are major capitalist institutions, their integration into the free-market system compels them to produce material that they think will sell.[8] In times of widespread skepticism about the merits of unfettered capitalism, the best way for movie moguls to make money may therefore be for them to produce pictures that give expression to that mass skepticism. The central thesis of this book is that the post-2011 period represents precisely such a moment. The films examined in this book can be perceived as cinematic expressions of popular discontent with global capitalism not in spite of, but at least in part *due to* their status as mass cultural products targeting an anonymous multitude.

I do not mean to suggest that studio executives wittingly erode the viewer's faith in the invisible hand of the free market in the movies they choose to produce. Nor do I make the claim that the filmmakers studied here expressly set out to allegorize the destruction of capitalism in their films. However, I do contend that cultural producers respond, to varying degrees and in widely divergent ways, to the world in which they live. Like many other cultural artifacts, movies absorb, process, and synthesize a society's hopes and fears at a given moment in time. This book explores the diverse ways that half a dozen films from the 2011–15 period do just that.

Rather than restricting the analysis to one national context, this study examines a cross section of films produced around the world in the early 2010s. Each of the films transposes this historical conjuncture into sounds and moving images in its own idiosyncratic way; as a composite, they form a fascinating collage of a particular moment in world history.

Year zero for this study is 2011, when a street protest in Tunisia set off a wave of demonstrations that spread from the Arab world to Europe and North America, eventually reaching every continent in the world. The movies under examination give audio-visual and narrative expression to that unprecedented global effervescence. The cosmopolitan selection of films reflects something of the international scope of that tumult, while the generic heterogeneity of the movies functions as an index of the broad spectrum of responses to the perpetuation of the politico-economic status quo after the revelation of the rot at the core of the system in 2008, when the dicey mortgage-backed securities that investment banks had been packaging and selling as though they were virtually risk-free suddenly became worthless, causing the worst global recession since the Great Depression of the 1930s.

The decision to center the study on movies of the post-recession period signals an important difference between the present work and the analyses proposed in books like Kirk Boyle and Daniel Mrozowski's *The Great Recession in Fiction, Film, and Television: Twenty-First Century Bust Culture* (2013), Alberto Toscano and Jeff Kinkle's *Cartographies of the Absolute* (2015), and my own *Rumble and Crash: Crises of Capitalism in Contemporary Film* (2019). To greater or lesser degrees, the latter books propose what Fredric Jameson calls "cognitive maps" of multinational capitalism.[9] Their common object of study is cultural figurations of global capital, not allegories of the end of capitalism. The event at their core is the global financial crisis of 2008, not the global revolts of 2011. Shifting the time frame forward a few years brings a new set of cultural artifacts into view. The movies examined in this book are less concerned with mapping the vicissitudes of multinational capitalism than they are with imagining the system's violent demise.

In hindsight, the time period covered in this book constitutes a distinct mini-sequence in the history of popular culture and the social attitudes it reflects. The anger and frustration that burst spectacularly into public view in 2011 has not disappeared, but it has taken new forms. On the right side of the political spectrum, discontent with the neoliberal status quo has fueled the rise of the far right in much of the Western world. In place of a vast and amorphous economic system, politicians and pundits on the right have offered discontented segments of the population with identifiable enemies—generally a socially marginalized minority of some sort—as outlets for their ire. This phenomenon is not new, as anyone with even a cursory familiarity with the history of fascism will recognize.[10] What is novel about the current situation is the extent to which the expansion of laissez-faire capitalism has continued unabated in tandem with the resurgence of the neo-fascist right. Meanwhile, the political left in capitalist-democratic states has channeled much of its energy into combating discriminatory attitudes, practices, and policies that have suddenly retaken center stage. Yet, as the culture wars of the late 2010s rage in city streets, on social media platforms, and in mainstream as well as niche news outlets, the neoliberal right's stealth class war continues apace. Far from being resolved, the issues raised in this book have entered into an even more critical phase since the early 2010s. In this context, the analyses that follow serve as a timely reminder that culture can and often does mediate movements in the global economy while issuing a renewed call to arms to people that may have momentarily retreated from the battle against the behemoth of multinational capitalism.

Chapter 1

The End of the World of the End: *Melancholia*

Lars von Trier's *Melancholia* (2011) is a rigorously structured film, divided into a prologue of roughly 7 minutes and two discrete parts of exactly 1 hour each. The movie's first part, called "Justine" after the character whose manically depressive nature gets the better of her, leading her to abandon her picture-perfect husband on their wedding night, quit her high-powered job in an advertising firm, and have a 30-second sexual encounter (filmed in real time) with an insignificant minor character, depicts one night in the life of a dysfunctional upper-class family. The second part, titled "Claire" after Justine's prim older sister, shows the two sisters' very different reactions to the impending end of terrestrial life as a massive rogue planet called Melancholia bears down upon the Earth. While Justine (Kirsten Dunst) grows calmer and increasingly serene as Melancholia approaches Earth, Claire (Charlotte Gainsbourg) emotionally disintegrates. These two narrative segments stand in radical opposition to one another. They present themselves as an audio-visual "thesis," on the one hand, and its violent antithesis, on the other. Whereas the first part, centered on Justine, depicts a decadent world of super-rich socialites whose petty intrigues the film probingly explores over the course of an hour, the second part, which shifts to Claire's perspective, proceeds to annihilate that world by sending a planetary mass on a collision course with Earth. "The world of *Melancholia* is a tiny, self-enclosed microcosm of Western white bourgeois privilege," Steven Shaviro writes in his penetrating analysis of the film; "and this microcosm is what gets destroyed at the end."[1]

This chapter interprets von Trier's apocalyptic vision of

the end of the world as an allegory of two contrasting ways of conceiving the end of time. On the one hand, the depiction of the idleness of the characters in the movie's first part offers a crystalline visualization of the "end of history" celebrated by Francis Fukuyama in his 1992 manifesto of the post-ideological world of triumphant neoliberalism, *The End of History and the Last Man*. Von Trier's detailed narration of his characters' frivolous adventures and his patient probing into their banal concerns serve to convey the vacuous existence of these super-rich jetsetters, who are presented as so many Nietzschean "last men" living in a Fukuyaman post-historical paradise. On the other hand, the second part presents a vision of the end of human time. Although the end of the world is brought about, in the film, by an arbitrary astronomical event, this event can be interpreted symptomatically, as a wish fulfillment condensing discontent with the Fukuyaman post-political world and willfully bringing about its conflagration in vivid color. If the first narrative thread, which I dub "the world of the end," finds its theoretical counterpart in the work of Fukuyama, the second, which I call "the end of the world of the end," finds its theoretical analog in Walter Benjamin's notion of divine violence and especially in Slavoj Žižek's appropriation of this powerful and provocative Benjaminian category.

Melancholia does not openly present itself as a political film. Its principal concern seems to be Justine's attempt to find meaning and purpose in relation to a family that does not understand her, a social milieu that alienates her, and a universe that overwhelms her. If I more or less bracket here the psychoanalytic, existential, and metaphysical dimensions of the movie in favor of a political reading, I do so for two reasons. First, although I find Fredric Jameson's affirmation that the political interpretation of texts is "the absolute horizon of all reading and all interpretation" hyperbolic, I agree with him that "the convenient working distinction between cultural texts that are social and political and those that are not" fails to account for the deep penetration of politics into private life and tacitly sanctions the idea that the individual artist or lone genius can somehow transcend his or her conjuncture—an idea that reinforces, intentionally or not, the fundamentally ideological idea that some of us are outside of ideology.[2] In sum, I agree with Jameson that cultural artifacts, whether they are explicitly "political" or not, can profitably be read as socially symbolic acts bearing witness to a "political unconscious." Second, I would argue that, appearances to the contrary, *Melancholia* is above all a political film, belonging to the first category of cultural texts that Jameson names: those that have explicitly social or political content. Although I do not mean to imply that the psychological, existential, and metaphysical aspects of the film are irrelevant in and of themselves, I will argue that the political interpretation of the film *renders* them irrelevant.

Unfathomable Profundity and Superficial Banality

Let us begin with the movie's stunning opening sequence. *Melancholia*'s prologue, which *New York Times* film critic Manohla Dargis calls "a masterpiece in miniature" in her extended analysis of the sequence, lasts the duration of Richard Wagner's overture to his 1865 opera, *Tristan und Isolde*.[3] It begins, in unison with the opening phrase of Wagner's haunting overture, with a fade-in from black to a huge close-up of Justine set just off center in the frame against a pinkish gray sky. Justine slowly opens her eyes and stares blankly at the camera as computer-generated images of birds and bats begin dropping gracefully out of the sky around her. The shot offers a miniature prelude to the film as a whole, juxtaposing Justine's spiritual awakening, depicted counterintuitively in the form of a vacant stare, and the impending apocalypse, represented in the lifeless creatures that fall from the sky.

The rest of the prologue consists primarily of super-slow-motion shots of characters in situations to which the film returns in the later narrative segments. An image of Justine dressed in the bridal gown and veil that she wears in the first part of the movie shows her floating downstream with a bouquet of lilies of the valley in her hands. We see her trudging through a forest glade with long, gray wooly tendrils clinging to her ankles and wrists. Additional shots of Justine sporting the jeans and T-shirt that she wears in the film's second part depict her with her arms outstretched as dragon flies and moths flurry around her, and looking inquisitively at her hands as electrostatic discharges emanate from her fingertips. We see Claire and her son, Leo (Cameron Spurr), trudging through a golf course, leaving deep imprints in the grass as they walk. The Flemish painter Pieter Breugel the Elder's *Hunters in the Snow* (1565) burns before our eyes in anticipation of the planetary destruction at the end of the film. A horse gently but inexorably collapses, an immaculately trimmed hedge is consumed by flames, and so forth. Intercut with these ground-level images are a series of outer-space shots of planets moving past each other and then colliding, completely destroying the smaller planet, Earth, as it collapses into the larger. The last shot of the prologue, which coincides with the crescendo of Wagner's overture, shows the reduction of the Earth to dust as it crashes into a planet more than ten times its size.

This prologue, which condenses the film's central motifs into a series of beautifully composed tableaux, gives pause for thought. Virtually all of the images in the sequence find an analogous moment in the body of the film, up to and including the collision of the two planets that consumes the biosphere in the movie's final frame. In an industry that places so much emphasis on producing audience-pleasing endings, von Trier's decision to begin the film by divulging the apocalyptic ending is remarkable. It flies in the face of one of the central tenets of narrative cinema: that the film should present a satisfying resolution to the narrative problems it raises.[4] If our main interest in the film lay in discovering what happened at the end, there would be no point in watching it. We know from the get-go how the story ends: the Earth is demolished; no one survives.

This revelation of the cataclysmic end right from the beginning also has the effect of making everything that follows seem pointless. The permutations of Justine's battle with depression are irrelevant given the imminent demise of the planet. The tensions between her and her newlywed husband become insignificant. Her conflict with her bigwig employer, the mixed emotions expressed between her and both her embittered mother and her alcoholic father, her emotional and physical dependence on a sister she disdains, and all of the myriad problems the heroine faces over the course of the film are revealed to be ultimately meaningless. All of these narrative tensions, which the film subtly probes over the course of 2 hours, have been stripped of their significance for the viewer who has already seen that all of this amounts to naught.

In a similar vein, von Trier's film style also undermines the viewer's interest in the development of the plot. Let us take an example. Following the prologue, the film narrative begins with a 3-minute scene of a limousine attempting to navigate its way along a winding dirt road. We see the car alternately inching forward and reversing while first the chauffeur, then Justine and her newlywed husband, Michael (Alexander Skarsgård), each try to move the limo past a tight bend in the road. This light-hearted scene, shot in a *Dogme 95* style with a handheld camera, natural lighting, and direct sound, in which Justine and Michael playfully interact with each other while the chauffeur nervously frets about his car, ends as abruptly as it begins, without showing whether the travelers overcome their obstacle. The scene is followed without transition by a shot of the bride and groom walking up a driveway to a château, where the wedding party awaits them. One assumes that the couple had to abandon the car on the road and hike the several miles to meet the wedding party (the change from one scene to the next from daylight to nighttime buttresses this interpretation), but one does not know and, frankly, does not really care. In contrast to similar uses of this editing technique, here the imbalance between the 3-minute scene during which, for all intents and purposes, nothing happens and the elliptical cut where the conflict is presumably resolved serves to undermine more than to generate our interest in the narrative.[5]

One could multiply examples of this sort. Von Trier's particular use of the jump cut, for instance, is the audio-visual equivalent of "etcetera." His propensity to open scenes with establishing shots *away* from which he immediately pans leads more to creating a sense of spatial confusion than to orienting the viewer in the narrative space. "The camera is handheld, and it flutters about continually, never staying still and never steadying itself, but instead continually indulging in swish pans, readjustments of focus, and nervous reframings," Shaviro observes. "There is often no functional reason for these movements," he continues. "It is as if the camera were suffering from that quintessential postmodern malady, attention deficit disorder."[6] The resolutely anticlimactic structure of the film is merely the most obvious example of von Trier's assault on cinematic conventions. However, if these breaches of cinematic convention have the general effect of undermining the spectator's interest in the development of the narrative, von Trier's probing camera, which lingers patiently on characters' faces in ways that invite us to enter into their inner world, produces the opposite effect. The result is a film characterized at the same time by an unfathomable profundity and an off-the-cuff superficiality.

One might propose a similar interpretation of the cataclysmic event that devours the world at the end of the film. In and of itself, such a conflagration would constitute the most decisive event in human history. But its function in the film can also be perceived as a cheap *deus ex machina* (a plot device whereby narrative problems are suddenly and abruptly resolved by the contrived intervention of some new event). The annihilation of the world at the end of the movie absolves von Trier of the responsibility of resolving or even seriously addressing the grave issues of human existence he evokes in the film.

If von Trier fails to shed much light on the deep metaphysical and existential questions that his film constantly invites us to ponder, the way an Ingmar Bergman or an Andrei Tarkovsky might, his film does lend itself to a far-reaching sociopolitical analysis. Indeed, following a Sartrean sort of "loser wins" logic, *Melancholia* succeeds in transmitting a socially and politically significant message to the precise extent that it fails to plumb the existential and metaphysical depths that it hints are just below the film's surface.[7]

The World of the End

The sociopolitical message of the film can be gleaned from a juxtaposition of its two main narrative segments. Following the scene of Justine and Michael attempting to maneuver the limo down the dirt road, the movie's first part narrates the newlyweds' wedding night. The wedding reception is "an obscenely lavish event, entirely worthy of the One Percent," Shaviro comments.[8] The décor is an opulent waterfront mansion with meticulously manicured grounds, complete with an 18-hole golf course, owned by Claire's billionaire husband, John (Kiefer Sutherland). The attire of the characters and the activities in which the wedding guests engage are in keeping with their ostentatious surroundings. Their fashionable clothing and especially the frivolous but ever-so-tasteful activities organized for the wedding party (the launch of fire balloons into the night sky, a midnight snack of onion soup served by a team of servants in black tie at a bleached-white tent set up for the purpose, and so forth) leave no doubt as to the family's social status. The film goes over the top in its depiction of the excesses of upper-class life. One almost feels as though one were watching an episode of *Lifestyles of the Rich and Famous*.

The latter show, which aired from 1984 to 1995 on US syndicated television, is a phenomenon of its times, spanning the transition from the Reagan–Bush years of the 1980s that saw the end of the Cold War and the emergence of the United States as the world's only superpower to the Clintonite 90s of bull markets, booming stock prices, and flush shareholders. There are many ways one might characterize this period of burgeoning global capitalism and the export of Western style democracy throughout the world. Perhaps the most compelling description of this era is the one proposed by political scientist Francis Fukuyama, an adviser to the Reagan White House and a key contributor to the so-called "Reagan Doctrine" in the 1980s, in his manifesto of the concomitant triumphs of neoliberal capitalism and liberal democracy in his 1992 book *The End of History and the Last Man*.

The overarching argument of Fukuyama's book is that the historical process, which began when the mythical "first men" engaged in armed combat for recognition by their opponents, has reached its endpoint. The argument draws heavily upon Alexandre Kojève's influential reading of GWF Hegel's theory of Universal History, proposed in a series of lectures at the École des Hautes Études in Paris between 1933 and 1939 during which Kojève read aloud and commented on Hegel's *Phenomenology of Spirit* (1807) line by line.[9] According to the interpretation of Universal History that Kojève puts forth in these lectures, history as such came to an end in 1806, when Napoléon Bonaparte, whom Hegel apparently saw ride past his house in Jena, marched triumphantly through Europe spreading what Kojève calls "the universal and homogeneous state."[10]

As Fukuyama clarifies, this idea that the historical process came to an end with the imposition of the French republican values of liberty and equality on the still largely feudal European continent at the beginning of the nineteenth century does not mean that "the natural cycle of birth, life, and death would end" or that "important events would no longer happen." What the theory of the end of history proposes is, rather, that "there would be no further progress in the development of underlying principles and institutions."[11] The theory is premised on the idea that human history is not just an accumulation of events but that it has a shape. It represents a fundamentally teleological vision of history, conceiving of social evolution as a logical progression advancing from simple tribal societies "through various theocracies, monarchies, and feudal aristocracies" to its ultimate endpoint, a terminus which it reached, according to Hegel, at the beginning of the nineteenth century.[12]

Fukuyama brings this theory to bear on global sociopolitical developments in the late twentieth century. If Hegel discerned the culmination of human history in the triumph of the French Emperor during the Napoleonic Wars, according to Fukuyama's updated version of the "end of history," the collapse of the Soviet Union and the Communist bloc in the late 1980s and early 1990s reflects "the achievement of a higher level of rationality on the part of those who lived in such societies, and their realization that rational universal recognition could be had only in a liberal social order."[13] In sum, the instauration of the New World Order represents, in Fukuyama's eyes, "the end point of human ideological evolution beyond which it [is] impossible to progress further."[14] History is over. With the fall of the Berlin Wall, all that remained was the "dénouement": the slow but inexorable colonization of the remaining pockets of resistance to Western style democracy.

For Fukuyama, this realization on the part of citizens of the former Communist bloc countries that human fulfillment can be attained only in liberal-democratic states (by which he means representative parliamentary democracies where people vote to elect their leaders) goes hand in hand with the conviction that only laissez-faire capitalism can deliver a satisfactory level of economic prosperity. While, on the one hand, "liberal democracy remains the only coherent political aspiration," on the other hand, "liberal principles in economics—the 'free market'—have succeeded in producing unprecedented levels of material prosperity."[15] These two forms of social progress—the political and the economic, democracy and capitalism—are intimately linked in Fukuyama's view: "A liberal revolution in economic thinking has sometimes preceded, sometimes followed, the move toward political freedom around the globe," he asserts, but whichever development comes first, it eventually brings the other one along with it.[16]

In his scathing critique of this argument in *Specters of Marx* (1993), Jacques Derrida calls attention to a recurrent slippage in Fukuyama's reasoning. The latter-day prophet of the end of history alternately presents the "good news" (Fukuyama's term) of history's end as a phenomenon that took place at the end of the Cold War and as a regulatory idea to guide future global developments: "Depending on how it works to his advantage and serves his purpose, Fukuyama defines liberal democracy here as an actual reality and there as a simple ideal."[17] Sometimes Fukuyama announces that liberal democracy and neoliberal capitalism swept the world in the last quarter of the twentieth century. At other times, he heralds the future realization of a global neoliberal democracy to come. The "good news" of the arrival of a system enabling the "limitless accumulation of wealth," accompanied by "an increasing homogenization of all human societies," is both our empirical present and our projected global future, Fukuyama alternately argues, where we currently are (in the early 1990s) and where we are heading (in the twenty-first century).[18]

I will return below to critique this Fukuyaman thesis and weigh its relevance in the current context, but I must say that I fundamentally agree with Žižek's 2008 assessment of the ongoing validity of Fukuyama's analysis as a descriptive model for understanding global developments into the first decade of the twenty-first century: "It is easy to make fun of Fukuyama's notion of the End of History, but the dominant ethos today *is* 'Fukuyaman': liberal-democratic capitalism is accepted as the finally found formula of the best possible society."[19] One may dislike Fukuyama's treatise or object to his smug tone, but it is hard to argue with the fact that, in the late twentieth and early twenty-first centuries, the world did seem to be approaching something of a consensus that, as Žižek says in another context, multinational neoliberalism is "the only game in town."[20]

Echoing Žižek, Mark Fisher writes in *Capitalist Realism* (2009): "Fukuyama's thesis that history has climaxed with liberal capitalism may have been widely derided, but it is accepted, even assumed, at the level of the cultural unconscious."[21] It is precisely this unconscious assumption of the inevitability of liberal capitalism—"the widespread sense that not only is capitalism the only viable political and economic system, but also that it is now impossible even to *imagine* a coherent alternative to it"—that Fisher calls "capitalist realism."[22] The implicit answer to the question posed in the subtitle to Fisher's book—*Is There No Alternative?*—is that there is none: "The 80s were the period when capitalist realism was fought for and established, when Margaret Thatcher's doctrine that 'there is no alternative'—as succinct a slogan of capitalist realism as you could hope for—became a brutally self-fulfilling prophecy."[23] One of the reasons that Fisher prefers the term "capitalist realism" to "postmodernism," Fredric Jameson's descriptor for the substantially similar phenomenon, is because the former term, unlike the latter, conjures the putative inevitability of global neoliberalism. "Jameson used to report in horror about the ways that capitalism had seeped into the very unconscious; now, the fact that capitalism has colonized the dreaming life of the population is so taken for granted that it is no longer worthy of comment," Fisher laments.[24] In sum, Fisher suggests, the end of history alternately announced and heralded by Fukuyama, the sense that "there is no alternative" to multinational capitalism and Western style democracy, has become a self-fulfilling prophecy that has saturated the political imagination to such a degree that it has become impossible even to envision a viable alternative to it. We therefore "find ourselves at the notorious 'end of history' trumpeted by Francis Fukuyama after the fall of the Berlin Wall," Fisher bitterly remarks 2 decades after the Berlin Wall fell.[25]

It is a visual crystallization of this post-historical world that the first part of *Melancholia* offers to the viewer. The fact that Justine works in the area of advertising, a post-historical profession if ever there was one, is a non-negligible detail in this regard. The image that we see of Justine's professional work leaves little doubt of the value that the film attributes to this sort of work. Justine's job would appear to consist primarily if not exclusively in coming up with taglines to accompany images (the one we see is that of three scantily clothed anorexic young women sprawled provocatively across a tile surface). Although Justine's cynical summary of her professional work (summed up in the question: "How do we effectively hook a group of minors on our substandard product, preferably in a habit-forming way?") is a hodgepodge of clichés that work at cross-purposes, the very excess of her critique seems designed to persuade the film audience of the evils of advertising and to elicit the viewer's disdain for the slice of life depicted on the screen.

It is also noteworthy that the two characters most directly linked to the post-historical worldview are treated with little sympathy in the film. Justine's boss, Jack (Stellan Skarsgård), the high-powered CEO of an advertising firm, is portrayed as a heartless taskmaster who thinks only about business, even on the wedding night of his most valued employee. Every scene in which he appears shows him either directly pressuring Justine to come up with the coveted tagline for the ad with the anorexic models or coercing his recently hired nephew (Brady Corbet) to extract it from her. When the hapless nephew fails to obtain the elusive tagline and Jack humiliates him by firing him in public, Justine puts into words the viewer's overall impression of the ambitious and obsessive CEO: "You are a despicable, power-hungry little man, Jack."

The other character directly tied to post-historical capitalism is Claire's husband, John, the owner of the magnificent property where the film action takes place and the sponsor of Justine and Michael's ostentatious wedding. In contrast to the single-minded Jack, who earns his money by exploiting his employees and whose business is to exploit the public, John is a super-rich socialite whose unfathomable wealth multiplies itself on the stock market without his having to do a day's work. John engages in two principal activities in the film. In the first part, his role consists primarily of reminding Justine and Claire how much money the wedding is costing him (although he also spends a good deal of time expressing his exasperation with Justine and his dislike for Claire and Justine's mother). In the second part of the movie, his primary narrative function is to reassure Claire that Melancholia will not collide with Earth. In both of these roles, he comes across as a self-assured master of the universe: metaphorically in the first instance, more literally in the second. He is a man who commands confidence. Like the technocrats who assure us that the stewardship of the global economy should be left to experts capable of understanding sophisticated mathematical models that the rest of us cannot possibly comprehend, John comes across as an authority on matters beyond the intellectual reach of the other characters in the film. The numerous shots of him observing Melancholia through his high-tech telescope and making calculations about the planet's anticipated path lend credence to his repeated assertions that Melancholia is not going to hit Earth. The irony, of course, is that he is dead wrong. The last shot we see of John—lying dead in a horse stable with his face in his own vomit after having consumed the poison that Claire bought in the event that his predictions were wrong—effectively communicates how much confidence von Trier thinks we should place in men of this sort.

Divine Violence

Whereas the first part of *Melancholia* lavishly details lifestyles of the rich and ostentatious, the second part proceeds to destroy the decadent world depicted in the first. I would read the cataclysmic event that brings about this end of the world of the end as a visualization of the sort of expiating violence that philosopher and cultural critic Walter Benjamin cryptically calls "divine" in his 1922 "Critique of Violence." The obscure Benjaminian category of divine violence, which designates a law-destroying violence directed against both law-preserving violence and the law-making violence that Benjamin identifies as "mythic," has generated an enormous amount of ink over the past few decades, giving rise to lively exchanges among such major thinkers as Giorgio Agamben, Judith Butler, Simon Critchley, Derrida, and Žižek.[26] For my purposes here, I will refer primarily to the remarks of Žižek, who proposes that "we should fearlessly identify divine violence with positively existing historical phenomena, thus avoiding any obscurantist mystification."[27]

Žižek poses "divine violence" as the counterforce to what he calls "systemic" violence. The latter form of violence, "the violence inherent in the system," includes "not only direct physical violence, but also the more subtle forms of coercion that sustain relations of domination and exploitation."[28] Divine violence, then, would be a sort of *Return to Sender*, a violence that turns systemic violence back in an inverted form on the system that produced it. So understood, divine violence would be a symptom, in the medical or psychoanalytic sense of the term, of the systemic violence necessary to maintain the way of life of those who benefit from a given socioeconomic configuration. Žižek offers the examples of the Jacobin Terror of 1793–94, the Red Terror of 1918–19, and the moment in the 1990s when the dispossessed of Rio de Janeiro descended from their *favelas* and started burning and looting the rich parts of the city like a swarm of Biblical locusts.[29] The latter example is particularly appropriate, for, as Žižek argues, in contrast to other forms of contestation, which may conceive of violence as a means to an end, divine violence "serves no means, not even that of punishing the culprits and thus re-establishing the equilibrium of justice. It is just a sign of the injustice of the world."[30]

The cataclysmic finale of *Melancholia* offers the viewer a spectacle of such apparently gratuitous destruction. Like Benjaminian divine violence, which strikes "without warning, without threat, and does not stop short of annihilation," the destruction of the Earth at the end of the film serves no purpose other than to stand as a complete and utter negation of the world portrayed on the screen.[31] Moreover, similar to Benjamin's sole example of divine violence—the passage from the Old Testament in which God punishes Korah and his followers for rebelling against him—at the end of the movie the world vanishes in a momentary flash that eliminates its every trace.[32] In the Biblical example, the Lord does not slaughter Korah and his retinue for their actions. Rather, "the ground that was under them split open, and the Earth opened its mouth and swallowed them, along with their households, and all Korah's men, and all their goods" (Numbers 16:30–32). As Critchley writes in his commentary on this Biblical example, "even the linen that was at the launderers and the needles borrowed by people at some distance from [Korah]" disappear. "Yahweh is nothing if not thorough."[33] Needless to say, the obliteration of every trace of the planet at the end of von Trier's film is no less thoroughgoing.

The Rebirth of History

One need only re-insert the film into its socio-historical context for the relevance of such an analysis to become immediately apparent. *Melancholia* came out in 2011, a year that bore witness to widespread discontent with the established world order. By Micah White's count, more than 150 protests, many of them occurring simultaneously in different locations, took place around the world during that year. According to White, a social activist, a co-editor of *Adbusters* magazine, and one of the core organizers of Occupy Wall Street, this figure represents "a doubling of protests with an identifiable grievance or explicit demand, from 59 in 2006 to 80 in 2008 and 153 in 2011."[34] The inaugural event that set off the year's cycle of revolts occurred in Tunisia on December 17, 2010, when Mohamed Bouazizi, a street vendor, set himself on fire at the gate of a provincial capital building to protest the humiliating treatment he had received at the hands of a police officer. "Bouazizi's death triggered immediate and widespread demonstrations, toppling the autocratic government of Ben Ali in Tunisia and igniting the Arab Spring."[35] The popular unrest spread quickly to Algeria, Yemen, Bahrain, Libya, and other countries in the Arab-speaking world, reaching its high point in Egypt, where tens of thousands of demonstrators gathered in Cairo's Tahrir Square to demand an end to President Hosni Mubarak's 30-year rule. Mubarak's resignation in February 2011 unleashed another wave of protests around the world. Inspired by the Tahrir Square uprising, 50,000 demonstrators calling themselves the *indignados*, or "angry ones," gathered on May 15 at the Puerta del Sol plaza in Madrid to protest their government's austerity budget. About 6 million of their compatriots (more than 13 percent of Spain's population) joined them as their 1-day march turned into a months-long encampment. Similar encampment protests took place at Syntagma Square in Athens, Greece, on the median of Rothschild Boulevard in Tel Aviv, Israel, and elsewhere.

Drawing inspiration from these global developments, a group of several thousand demonstrators descended on Wall Street in September of the same year to express their discontent with a global situation in which 1 percent of the world's population possessed as much wealth as the other 99 percent combined. By mid-October, Occupy protests had occurred or were currently underway in nearly a thousand cities around the world.

In his 2011 "Person of the Year" article dedicated to "the protestor" in *Time* magazine, Kurt Andersen, summing up the year's events, declares that 2011 was "unlike any year since 1848, when one street protest in Paris blossomed into a three-day revolution that [...] inspired an unstoppable cascade of protest and insurrection" across Europe.[36] As philosopher Alain Badiou, who also discerns echoes of the European revolutions of 1848 in the uprisings of 2011, writes in *The Rebirth of History*—a title that should be heard with all its anti-Fukuyaman resonance—"we find ourselves in a *time of riots* wherein a rebirth of History [...] is signalled and takes shape."[37] Žižek, for his part, who dubs 2011 "the year of dreaming dangerously," argues that the year's popular insurrections carry an overarching message: "We do not live in the best possible world."[38] Countering the Thatcher doctrine, which had reigned for 3 decades, that "there is no alternative" to multinational capitalism, in Žižek's view, the mobilizations of 2011 showed that, at long last, "we are allowed, obliged even, to think about the alternatives."[39] In sum, 2011 bore witness to a collective desire for the end of the end of history.

The End of Protest?

The various protest movements enumerated above obviously expressed diverse grievances and made different sets of demands, but they all had some identifiable grievance or discernable demand. Even the Occupy movement, which refrained from articulating a coherent message or setting out a clear set of demands, was quite consciously protesting the gross

27

inequalities of wealth and power that the current parliamentary-capitalist system fosters. The situation is different in the case of the riots that erupted in cities across the United Kingdom in August of 2011. "Similar to the riots in the Paris suburbs in 2005," Žižek writes, "the UK protestors had no message to deliver."[40] In contrast to the uprisings that took place in Cairo, Madrid, New York, and elsewhere, these "'zero-level' protests," as Žižek calls them, had no content beyond their negation of the world that the protestors inhabited.[41] Like the poor residents of Rio that descended onto the bourgeois neighborhoods like a plague of locusts in the 1990s, the thousands of rioters who burned and looted cities across England in the summer of 2011 had no explicit political agenda. Their violent outbursts demanded nothing, not even justice for Mark Duggan, the Tottenham resident whose murder by police sparked the violence. The riots were an impotent expression of rage that turned into a weeklong carnival of destruction. Like Benjaminian divine violence, which (as seen above), in Žižek's powerful and timely reading, "serves no means, not even that of punishing the culprits and thus re-establishing the equilibrium of justice," the UK riots were "pure means," which is to say, a means without an end.[42]

In relation to riots like the ones that took place in England in 2011, Žižek writes that "if the commonplace that we live in a post-ideological era has any sense at all, it is here, in these ongoing outbursts of violence, that it becomes discernible."[43] Drawing a general conclusion from this particular example, Žižek proposes that "the more a society conforms to a well-organized rational state, the more the abstract negativity of 'irrational' violence returns."[44]

Žižek's diagnosis here should serve as a word of warning. As White observes in his autopsy of the Occupy movement, this mass demonstration had all the ingredients of a traditionally successful protest: "Occupy was mass, modern, secular [...] and overwhelmingly non-violent."[45] It was, in his estimation, "nearly a textbook example of a movement that should work."[46] Yet, White is forced to admit, the movement changed nothing: "We did not bring an end to the influence of money on democracy, overthrow the corporatocracy of the 1 percent or solve income inequality."[47] On the contrary, the situation has deteriorated since the days of the Occupy movement. According to an Oxfam report released in 2015, it was actually not true in 2011 that 1 percent of the global population controlled as much wealth as the rest of the world combined, but it is now.[48] In other words, the state of affairs decried by the protestors in Zuccotti Park has gotten worse, not better, since Occupy Wall Street.

During the twentieth century, White recalls, Western leaders felt compelled to respond to overwhelming demonstrations of popular discontent. In the twenty-first century, he observes, politicians in the West no longer seem to feel a need to listen to their constituents. In the face of intense international pressure from protestors, leaders of virtually all the advanced Western capitalist-democratic states chose simply to ignore the message that was being delivered and to continue bolstering a perverse system that, since 2011, has enabled the 62 richest people on the planet to garner as much of the world's wealth as the poorest 50 percent.[49] Despite the explosion of popular discontent around the world in 2011, we have not brought about the end of the end of history, far from it.

The spectacular failure of the Occupy movement leads White to the conclusion that the era of social protest is over, at least in the West.[50] Mass demonstrations no longer work to sway leaders of democratic states in the twenty-first century, he concludes. In response to critics who suggest that if the Occupy protestors had clearly articulated a specific goal, their movement may have had a greater impact (and therefore, that it is the lack of a clear demand that is in question, not social protest as such), White reminds his readers that the global march on February 15, 2003 against the invasion of Iraq, the largest protest event in human history, failed to sway US President George W. Bush and British Prime Minister Tony Blair to halt their pre-emptive war on Iraq.[51] The demand not to invade Iraq is as simple, straightforward, and clearly articulated a message as one could hope for, and yet Bush and Blair simply shrugged it off and went ahead with the invasion. Thinking about the ineffectiveness of these massive twenty-first-century protests, it is hard not to conclude that White is onto something, and that we may indeed have reached "the end of protest."

Although White recognizes that, in view of its lack of tangible results, Occupy Wall Street was a failure, he considers it to be a "constructive failure" rather than a total failure. In his opinion, there are valuable lessons to be learned from the Occupy experiment. The biggest lesson that he took away from his involvement in the movement is that we have to reinvent social activism. "So, what does this new paradigm of activism look like?" he asks. "It is defined by a shift away from materialist theories of social change toward a spiritual understanding of revolution. It is a turn from voluntarism and structuralism toward subjectivism and theurgism."[52] In sum, White proposes, the failures of the great protest movements of the twenty-first century have taught us that we need to hope for divine intervention.

White is quite explicit about this appeal to divine authority: "Activists of tomorrow will abandon strict secularism and materialism in favour of a nuanced approach that embraces theurgy and the yearning for divine intercession."[53] The author clarifies in his book that he was not a believer during his formative years. As he recounts, one of his formative experiences as a budding activist in the late 1990s was to engage in a nationally publicized battle against his high school's administration in order to found an atheist student club.[54] It is the time in which we live, White suggests—a time when popular manifestations of collective will have proven to be ineffectual means of social

30

engagement in so-called democratic states—that compels us to seek the intercession of a divine force in order to change the course of human history.

White is not alone in calling for a turn to theology in order to reinvigorate grassroots politics. On the contrary, his book finds its place alongside a growing number of studies that call for an integration of theology into political theory and practice. Recent publications such as Agamben's *The Time that Remains* (2005), John Gray's *Black Mass: Apocalyptic Religion and the Death of Utopia* (2007), Terry Eagleton's *Reason, Faith, and Revolution* (2009), Žižek's *Living in the End Times* (2010), and Critchley's *The Faith of the Faithless: Experiments in Political Theology* (2012) are just some noteworthy examples of this trend. Although White is an activist rather than an academic, whose book is focused on practical modes of engagement instead of theoretical analysis, his call for a form of activism that "embraces theurgy and the yearning for divine intercession" is part of a larger trend, which has swept academia in recent decades.

Critchley gives an especially concise justification for this phenomenal return of religion in left-wing politics in recent years. In the opening pages of *The Faith of the Faithless* he asks: "Is politics conceivable without religion? The answer is obviously affirmative as the evidence of various secular political theories testifies. But is politics *practicable* without religion? [...] I do not think so."[55] This is a remarkable statement. Politics is impracticable without religion. Critchley's position here is particularly surprising given his own professed atheism and especially given the grave concerns he expresses about the infusion of religion into politics that is currently taking place in the world. "We are living through a chronic re-theologization of politics," he writes, "which makes this time certainly the darkest period in my lifetime."[56] Clichés about the hair of the dog—or the god—that bit you come to mind. If the theologization of politics is a dangerous phenomenon defined by the violence and intolerance one finds in the religious fundamentalisms that have taken hold of large sectors of the world's population, then the solution to the problem, Critchley tells us, is to be sought in re-theologizing politics.

Critchley concludes his quite impressive study—which is both a timely and compelling critical analysis of the role of religion in political theory and practice, on the one hand, and a not altogether convincing attempt to theologize politics, on the other—with an examination of Benjaminian divine violence. "What is divine about divine violence?" he asks in the closing pages of his book. "The name 'God' is not the super-juridical source of the moral law. On the contrary, 'God' is the first anarchist."[57] Critchley could almost be talking here about the absent "god in the machine" in *Melancholia*, the one that wipes the slate clean at the end of the movie in a ruthless act of expiating violence that swallows the world whole. "Divine violence is lethal and it annihilates," Critchley writes in reference to Benjamin, "but it also expiates: it is *entsühnend*, atoning or cleansing like the use of water in a religious ritual."[58]

Although he does not reference it, Critchley's remarks here read like an inadvertent demonstration of Fredric Jameson's famous maxim that "it is easier to imagine the end of the world than to imagine the end of capitalism."[59] Originally coined in *The Seeds of Time* (1994), where Jameson proposes that "the word *postmodernism* ought to be reserved for thoughts of this kind," Jameson's dictum about it being easier today to imagine the end of the world than to envision a world without capitalism has become a catchphrase on the left.[60] Žižek has repeated the slogan with such frequency in books, articles, and interviews that it has become one of his signature bywords.[61] Fisher uses the phrase to convey what he means by "capitalist realism."[62] The slogan has come to typify the impasse of the anti-capitalist left at the dawn of the twenty-first century. *Melancholia* urges us to ponder why this is so. Rather than providing yet another example showing that Jameson et al. are right, von Trier's film proposes an implicit *interpretation* of Jameson's watchword, not only enabling us to appreciate, once again, that it is easier today to imagine the destruction of the planet than the breakdown of global capitalism but beckoning us to consider *why* this is so.

By patiently detailing the frivolity and vacuity of a group of super-rich masters of the universe and then proceeding to demolish their world (and ours) in an act of divine violence, von Trier both conveys the moral bankruptcy of members of the upper class and offers a fantasy vision of their demise. However, if *Melancholia* offers no viable alternative to the decadent world it depicts on the screen, if the only solution it proposes to the dead-end of post-history is a makeshift *deus ex machina* that engulfs the world, this lack of political imagination may itself be a sign of the times. At a moment when the most serious challenge to the capitalist-parliamentary world order is posed by the resurgence of religious fundamentalisms—a time when even some of the most committed radicals on the left are starting to conceive of the poison as a cure—where do critics of the inexorable advances of global capitalism turn? As the avenues for substantial social change are progressively closed off by the hegemony of multinational capital and the liberal-democratic institutions that support it, the political imagination is thwarted in its attempt to imagine a viable alternative. In the context of the decades-long reign of the "end of history," which has culminated, if White's diagnosis is correct, in a concomitant "end of protest," the idea of a tabula rasa that razes the system to the ground starts to become easier to imagine than a more modest transformation of the mechanisms of multinational neoliberalism. It is, finally, to this political impasse that von Trier's *Melancholia* attests. "If the world ends, then at least we will be freed from the rapacity of financial institutions, and from our ever-increasing burdens of debt," Shaviro quips.[63] As a utopian vision of a post-capitalist world, this is about the best that von Trier has to offer.

Fortunately, although von Trier gets the first word here, he does not get the last. David Cronenberg's *Cosmopolis* offers a very different vision of the demise of neoliberalism.

Chapter 2

The Demise of Finance Capital: *Cosmopolis*

Whereas the allegorical dimensions of *Melancholia* come into view from a macro-perspective, bracketing the intricacies of the plot and contemplating the movie's overarching narrative structure, the allegorical thrust of David Cronenberg's *Cosmopolis* (2012), based on Don DeLillo's 2003 novel of the same title, is transmitted first and foremost through details of the plot. This chapter begins therefore with an interpretation of the ways that the film narrative allegorizes the end of capitalism. Following the itinerary of the movie's protagonist, Eric Michael Packer (Robert Pattinson), the reckless billionaire asset manager whose downfall the film chronicles, the chapter argues that the film gives narrative expression to the widespread mistrust of and resentment toward the bankers and hedge fund managers who crashed the global economy in 2008. This antipathy is in turn personified, in the film, by Richard Sheets aka Benno Levin (Paul Giamatti), a former currency analyst at Packer Capital now cast into poverty and irrelevance who kills the tycoon at the end of the movie. Sheets is driven to murder not by a sense of moral purpose or political commitment, but due at least in part to the profound sense of alienation that he feels from his work. In Marxian terms, whereas Packer is a representative or "bearer" (*Träger*) of capitalism, Sheets suffers from a contemporary form of the *Entfremdung* that the young Marx associated with industrial labor. However, Sheets is emblematic of the plight of labor in more ways than one. In addition to experiencing a particularly neoliberal form of alienated labor, he is also made redundant by a digital technology that computes faster than he can think. He therefore finds himself among the swelling ranks of the twenty-first-century unemployed. In this context, Sheets' murder of Packer at the end of the film comes across as a violent return not of the repressed, but of the alienated and discarded.

The chapter is also concerned with thinking about how the film functions audio-visually and dramatically as well as narratively and thematically. Watching *Cosmopolis* is a strange experience. Cronenberg, who wrote the screenplay in addition to directing the film, makes little effort to draw the spectator into the narrative or encourage her to identify with the characters on the screen. On the contrary, the film continually distances us from the dramatic action unfolding before our eyes. In a manner reminiscent of the great European avant-garde playwrights of the twentieth century, most especially Bertolt Brecht, Cronenberg's film encourages us to think rather than to feel. *Cosmopolis* is designed to provoke an intellectual rather than an emotional response. Examining the array of cinematic and dramatic "estrangement" techniques that the screenwriter-director and his cast and crew use in the film, this chapter shows how *Cosmopolis* extends a twentieth-century tradition of engaged avant-garde theater into the realm of twenty-first-century film.

Death of a Financier

There is little obvious narrative development in the first hour of *Cosmopolis*. As Packer's luxury stretch limousine sits at a virtual standstill in dense cross-town traffic, the financier holds court from his throne at the back of the car to a cast of characters who meet with him to discuss such topics as finance, cyber-security, the future of capitalism, his short position on the Chinese yuan, his art collection, and his favorite rapper. The young trader crosses paths with his newlywed wife, Elise (Sarah Gadon), on three occasions, and he is in constant contact with his chief of security (Kevin Durand), but the plot advances at a pace not much faster than the limo. Yet as the car inches forward, so does the plot, and a coherent narrative begins to emerge. This first subchapter proposes a thumbnail film synopsis showing how the movie's central storyline and its principal themes gradually take form.

The film's MacGuffin is the young CEO's desire for a haircut.[1] Packer wants his chauffeur to drive him across town from his residence in Midtown East to a family barbershop in Hell's Kitchen, on the west side of Manhattan, so he can get a trim. This 12-block trip across town ends up taking all day. Packer leaves for his destination at breakfast time and arrives at the barber's after nightfall.

Traffic is held up due principally to three events taking place in Midtown. First, the US president's visit to New York has, in the words of Packer's omnipresent chief of security, "deleted entire streets from the map." Next, the limo encounters a massive anti-capitalist street protest in the neighborhood of Times Square. Finally, as evening approaches, a funeral procession for Brutha Fez, a fictional Sufi rap star, impedes the car's progress.

Interwoven with these three traffic-jam narratives are three assassination scenarios. Early in the film, the ubiquitous chief of security informs his boss of "a credible threat" on the US president's life. "This means a ride cross-town does not happen unless we make a day of it, with cookies and milk," the bodyguard advises his employer. The CEO's response to this information is telling: "Do people still shoot at presidents?" Packer asks. "I thought there were more stimulating targets." These short sentences succinctly communicate a worldview in which political figures have lost the power and prestige that once made them prime assassination targets. Implicit in Packer's offhand remark is the idea that a new set of figures has supplanted heads of state as the putative powerbrokers of the world. The film's second two assassination targets indicate the field of influence of these new masters of the universe. The first of these two figures is Arthur Rapp, the managing director of the International Monetary Fund (IMF), who is ambushed during a live interview on North Korean television. The second is the chief executive officer of Packer Capital, Eric Packer himself.

Whereas the three street-level encounters belong respectively to the political, social, and cultural registers, the three assassination scenarios belong to the political sphere, in the first case, and to the world of finance and economics in the other two cases. Significantly, only the latter two of these three mortal threats materialize in the film. Whereas the allegedly "credible threat" to the president's safety disappears without comment from the film narrative, Director Rapp is murdered onscreen, and the movie's long closing sequence shows that the threat on Packer's life is very real indeed. To this extent, the film shares Packer's view that there are "more stimulating targets" than political leaders. The world of *Cosmopolis* is a world in which the financial managers of the world rule the day. "People eat and sleep in the shadow of what we do," Packer's head of technology tells the CEO early in the movie. There is nothing in the film to suggest that this assessment is inaccurate.

The film recasts this shift from the narrowly defined political sphere to the realm of high finance in a slapstick parody of assassination enacted by André Petrescu (Mathieu Amalric), the self-proclaimed "pastry assassin," who hits Packer in the face with a cream pie an hour into the film. Petrescu, who claims that his "mission worldwide" is "to sabotage power and wealth," informs the whipped-cream-covered CEO that he passed up an attack on the president of the United States in order to strike him. "You are major statement," the gloating pastry assassin informs his cream-pie victim by way of explanation. Joining the ranks of such real-life cream-pie targets as neoliberal guru Milton Friedman, IMF Director Michel Camdessus, Microsoft's Bill Gates, and media baron Rupert Murdoch,[2] the fictional Eric Packer is elevated, by association, to the status of one of the most influential powerbrokers of our time: one worthy not only of a "pastry assassination" but, the film suggests, of an actual assassination as well.

The author of Packer's actual assassination is Richard Sheets, who murders the asset manager in the movie's last scene. In fact, this final scene cuts from a shot of Sheets holding his victim at gunpoint to the closing credits, leaving open the possibility that the assassin does not pull the trigger. Like DeLillo's novel, which ends with the murderer "waiting for the shot to sound," the film ends with Sheets' gun trained at the financier's head.[3] However, at this point in the film, Packer is no longer really alive anyway. Cronenberg suggests as much in the director's commentary on the Entertainment One DVD. "You don't actually have to kill him," the director asserts. "He's already dead."[4] Let us take a moment to sketch in broad strokes this metaphorical death.

The downfall of Packer that transpires over the course of the film takes two forms, one physical and the other financial. In both cases, the ruin is self-inflicted. On the financial level, we learn early in the movie that Packer has leveraged a great deal of capital in order to maximize profits from a bet he placed on the devaluation of the Chinese yuan. As it turns out, the inflated currency does not fall, and the speculator's high-stakes bet results in his maximizing his losses.

As the past few decades of economic history have made abundantly clear, this sort of risky behavior is far from uncommon in the era of advanced neoliberalism. Whereas DeLillo's novel, published in 2003, would call to mind such events as the bursting of the dot-com bubble in 2000 and the Enron bankruptcy of 2001, Cronenberg's film, released in 2012, brings most readily to mind the crash of the mortgage bond market in 2008 and the Great Recession that ensued. In sum, the fictional Packer is by no means an aberration in the world of high finance. On the contrary, his risky high-stakes bet is more emblematic than it is anomalous.

Packer's physical demise occurs in tandem with his financial ruin. As the news of the yuan's stubborn refusal to drop recurs throughout the film, the asset manager engages in increasingly irrational behavior. The first indication that Packer may be as fascinated by the prospect of his self-destruction as he is motivated by his self-interest occurs during his first encounter with the anti-capitalist protestors parading through the streets of Midtown. Two demonstrators enter into the restaurant where Eric and his wife, Elise, are having lunch. The two demonstrators each raise a pair of dead rats that they dangle from their tails, and they chant a modified version of the opening line of Marx and Engels' *Communist Manifesto*: "A specter is haunting the world! A specter is haunting the world! A specter is haunting the world!" They then fling the rats into the four corners of the restaurant and run out the door. At this point, the scene cuts to a shot of the cook behind the counter, who is brandishing a carving knife as if to attack the pesky renegades, and then to a medium close-up of Packer, who smiles with amusement as he watches the fleeing protestors. Rather than perceiving these rabble-rousers as a threat, a nuisance, or an irrelevance, Packer displays curiosity about, even admiration for these anti-capitalist agitators and their little piece of agitprop theater. Although the film does not belabor the point, the object of the demonstrators' ire is precisely people like Packer, who is a flesh-and-blood incarnation of the system they oppose. The tycoon's fascination with these protestors is therefore implicitly an attraction to his would-be assassins, who would negate the system that makes Packer the man he is even if they would not necessarily eliminate the man himself.

The following sequence obeys a similar logic. In it, we see Packer and his "chief of theory" (Samantha Morton), cocooned in the opulent Packer limousine, wax poetic about techno-capital and "creative destruction" while a band of street protestors vandalize the car. As the demonstrators trash the limo, Packer watches them from inside the car with detached amusement. A subsequent scene, toward the end of the film, during which Packer urinates in the back of the car, shows the financier playing an active role in the demolition that he passively admires here.

The urination shot directly follows a sequence in which Packer nonchalantly shoots his chief of security in the head, as if on a whim, before throwing the gun over a fence and into a basketball court where two kids are playing one-on-one. Given that the primary role in the film of the now dead bodyguard was to protect Packer from a "specific and categorical" threat on the billionaire's life, this off-handed execution constitutes a willful self-exposure to danger as well as an act of gratuitous violence. Exposing himself even more overtly to danger at the end of the film, Packer is drawn into Sheets' lair by a volley of shots fired at him from an abandoned warehouse. His entrance into the derelict building is therefore tantamount to a courtship with death if not an act of outright suicide. And before Sheets–Levin shoots (or aims to shoot) his nemesis in the head, the CEO impulsively fires a shot into the back of his own hand. From a reckless bet placed on an overvalued currency and a fascination with the would-be authors of his financial destitution to Packer's self-mutilation and finally his submission to an execution-style murder, the film charts the conscious self-destruction of its primary character.

Allegorizing the Bearers of Capitalism

As numerous commentators have suggested, *Cosmopolis'* Eric Packer is not really a "character" in the way that, say, Gordon Gekko (Michael Douglas) in Oliver Stone's *Wall Street* (1987), Ryan Bingham (George Clooney) in Jason Reitman's *Up in the Air* (2009), or the title characters of John Wells' *The Company Men* (2010) are. The film is not interested in Packer's psychological motivations, his inner turmoil, or his particular traits, drives, motives, or ambitions. As Kirk Boyle remarks in his incisive study of *Cosmopolis* and Dan Gilroy's *Nightcrawler* (2014), "Our care about what happens to Packer [...] is not tied to his fate as a flesh-and-blood character but to his fortune as a political-economic ideology incarnate."[5] Both the stilted dialog, which, in the words of *New Yorker* film critic Richard Brody, "has a technical chill, like that of the speech of robots imitating humans," and the performance of Robert Pattinson, who, as Caetlin Benson-Allott observes, "limits the movement of his facial features, precluding false attributions of interiority," have the effect of turning Packer into an automaton.[6]

Boyle offers a brilliant reading of this robotic inhumanity of *Cosmopolis'* main character. Charting the evolution post-1968 of the ideology of "capitalism with a human face," in which a cold and faceless system variously adopts the masks of charity, social responsibility, and playfulness, Boyle wittily argues that "*Cosmopolis* and *Nightcrawler* reverse the conventional plot of the famous cartoon *Scooby Doo*. Instead of unmasking a monster to reveal a deviant person, these films unmask a human to reveal a monstrous system."[7] What these films do, in Boyle's interpretation, is "depict capitalism with a human face as an impossibility."[8]

This sharp critique of capitalism with a human mask recalls the allegorical role that the capitalist plays in Karl Marx's writings. In contrast to the workers, who are dominated and exploited by the owners of private capital, the latter are the "representatives" or "bearers" (*Träger*) of capitalism.[9] "From the very beginning," Fredric Jameson writes in *Representing Capital*, "Marx's allegorical sense warned us that capitalists are to be considered but *Träger* of the process and not subjects (something he never says about the proletariat), even though they are also its beneficiaries."[10] Rather than being human agents per se, "the capitalists were mere allegorical figures, mere bearers, or *Träger*, of structure and of system."[11]

Jameson contrasts this allegorical role that the capitalist plays in Marx's writings with "older allegories," which present an "anthropomorphic character who 'represented' something, an idea or a value, whose name it wears on its back, as though to announce: 'I am Greed! I am Virtue!'"[12] In Jameson's view, "the depersonalizing pressure of the modern [...] dissolves these centered subjectivities in much the same way as, for Marx, the replacement of the tool by the machine transforms the worker from the master into the servant of the impersonal process."[13] With the exception of what Jameson calls "a few memorable cameos" (including "the sycophantic Senior, the abominable Duchess of Southerland, the unhappy Mr Peel"), the allegorical role that the capitalist plays in Marx's work is that of a depersonalized "bearer" of an economic process.[14]

The Eric Packer of Cronenberg's film comes across as an allegory (in the older sense) of this modern allegorical figure. A flesh-and-blood prosopopoeia, the robotic manager gives a face to a faceless system, but one which, as Boyle shows, the film presents as a *mask*. Cronenberg's wooden dialog and Pattinson's bloodless performance have the effect not only of presenting us with a two-dimensional allegorical figure, but of simultaneously showing us that what this figure represents is itself allegorical. Packer allegorizes an allegory, if you will, providing an audio-visual trope for the impersonal "bearers" of a mechanistic process. It is as though he were wearing a sandwich sign that reads not "I am Greed!" or "I am Virtue!" but "I am Allegory!" Intentionally or not, the blank mask that Pattinson dons for the role and the hollow dialog that Cronenberg scripts for the character communicate beautifully the intrinsically allegorical function that Marx imputes to the capitalist.

Returning now to the fate that this *Träger* suffers in the film narrative, the self-destruction of the financier takes on a broader relevance than the personal drama of a particular character. Coinciding with the publication of books with titles like *Saving Capitalism* (Robert Reich) and *Saving Capitalism and Democracy* (Mohamed Rabie), at a time when Thomas Piketty's *Capital in the Twenty-First Century*—which concludes with a detailed 99-page plan to save capitalism from itself—occupied the number one spot on the *New York Times* Best Seller list, while Nobel Prize-winning economists like Paul Krugman and Joseph Stiglitz were urgently proposing ways to prevent the bearers of capitalism from shooting themselves in the foot (or the hand), Cronenberg's narrative of the self-destruction of an allegorical embodiment of the system resonates more deeply than the story of a particular individual's fate.

Given that, following the 2008 meltdown, the *Träger* of the system have not heeded the advice of these Cassandras of late neoliberalism, *Cosmopolis* remains as timely today as when it was released. The massive US government bailout, in September 2008, of the very institutions that brought the global economy to the brink of collapse set the course for the response to the financial crisis. Forced to choose between bailing out the profiteers whose reckless behavior caused the debacle and helping the rest of the population survive the crisis, the government made the predictable choice and bailed out the financiers with taxpayer money, to the tune of $700 billion in cash and the promise of trillions more in the form of government guarantees for "toxic assets" still on the banks' books. This undisguised gift to the institutions that crashed the global economy was made without breaking up the banks that had been deemed "too big to fail," without demanding that these institutions change significantly their business practices, and without passing legislation that would prevent a repeat performance of the 2008 meltdown. We therefore find ourselves "tumbling inexorably toward the next great catastrophe—the only real question being how long it will take."[15] In sum, although the fictional Eric Packer comes to a bloody end, his empirical counterparts in the real world are alive and thriving. These real-life *Träger* are free to continue leveraging astronomical sums of money to place risky bets on volatile financial instruments with the tacit assurance that if they are big enough and their losses extreme enough, the taxpayers will bail them out.

Modes of Estrangement

As the foregoing synopsis of Packer's downfall suggests, *Cosmopolis* can be neatly divided into two distinct acts. The first hour of the film is set largely in Packer's limousine as it inches its way across Manhattan at a snail's pace. The last half-hour or so takes place outside the limo. These two film segments look and feel very different, and they show contrasting facets of contemporary capitalism. Packer's exit from the limo marks aesthetic and dramatic shifts as well as a narrative transition in the film. I propose here to look first at the first narrative segment, which I place under the heading of "estrangement" (*Verfremdung*), then at the second part of the film, which falls under the twin headings of "alienation" (*Entfremdung*) and "immiseration." Inserted between these two subsections is a short excursus on leveraging fictitious capital.

Packer's trip across town, an hour of screen time that corresponds to roughly 12 hours of narrative time, is broken up by the visit of half a dozen consultants and associates who enter and exit the limo to meet with the trader. Shiner (Jay Bucharel), Packer Capital's head of technology, assures the CEO that their system is secure. Michael Chin (Philip Nozuka), the company's systems analyst, expresses concern that Packer is "leveraging too rashly." Didi Fancher (Juliette Binoche), an art dealer and Eric's lover, attempts to persuade her client-lover that it is socially irresponsible for him to buy the Rothko Chapel, an octagonal non-denominational place of worship containing 14 Mark Rothko paintings, and sequester it in his private residence. Jane Melman (Emily Hampshire), chief of finance, repeats the concern that they have "a yuan carry that could crush us in hours." She is also present for Packer's daily prostate exam, clenching her water bottle as her employer submits to his ritual rectal examination conducted in limo by a doctor with latex gloves. Vija Kinsky (Samantha Morton), Packer's chief of theory, muses about the temporality of cyber-capitalism as a swarm of street protestors rock the billionaire's limousine and cover it with spray paint. Finally, Kosmo Thomas (Goûchy Boy), Brutha Fez's manager, informs Eric that the Brutha has died of cardiac arrest and commiserates with the disconsolate billionaire, whose only display of emotion in the movie occurs when he breaks down in tears at the news of the rapper's death.

Each of these encounters in the limousine unfolds like a discrete mini-episode. Cronenberg's use of the clean cut (as opposed to dissolves, fade-outs, fade-ins, and the like) for every shot transition in the film and his avoidance of establishing shots that would serve the dual function of signaling a scene change and situating the viewer in the narrative space, have the effect of plunging the viewer directly into the scenes, which begin almost invariably *in medias res*. The filmmaker does not add either diegetic or non-diegetic sound cues that would punctuate the scenes either by marking their beginning or signaling their ending. As a result of these various cinematic devices (or lack thereof), the scenes cannot really be said to begin or end; rather, they just start and then abruptly stop.

Moreover, there is little narrative development within the individual scenes. One senses that the dialog in many of the limo scenes could be rearranged with our barely noticing. Both within the individual scenes and between them, the film's first hour seems to unfold in a time out of time. We see Packer have breakfast, lunch, and dinner; daylight yields to nighttime; yet these indications of the passage of time fail to compensate for the temporal dislocation that the spectator experiences while watching the film.

This temporal dislocation works in tandem with a spatial disorientation, which begins from the movie's opening shot. The film, like the novel, is set in New York City. Yet the movie's first image, a long tracking shot filmed on location at the grand entryway of Toronto's Union Station, situates us in a city that is visibly other than it purports to be. For those unfamiliar with

Toronto's main train station, it is worth mentioning that Union Station is not a non-descript edifice. On the contrary, it is an iconic landmark, as recognizable as any low-rise building in the city. As far as high-rises are concerned, the city's most distinctive structure is undoubtedly the CN Tower, which dominates the Toronto skyline the way the Eiffel Tower dominates Paris or the Space Needle dominates Seattle. Its inclusion in the background of the basketball-court scene cannot fail to signal to the viewer that, diegesis to the contrary, we are in Ontario's capital city. Finally, as Amy Taubin notes in her characteristically smart and perceptive film review in *Artforum*: "Through the limo's windows, we glimpse what is recognizably Toronto—not, as in Hollywood movies that shoot in Canada to save money, Toronto disguised as New York, but Toronto as Toronto disorientingly referred to as New York."[16]

Kirk Boyle, who also cites this observation by Taubin, interprets this incongruity between the nominal New York and the empirical Toronto as a filmic creation of a "global city" (a term Boyle borrows from sociologist Saskia Sassen) in an era when metropolises around the world are coming to resemble each other more and more. It is a fascinating interpretation. What I want to emphasize here is the way that the disjunction between the movie's setting and its filming locations forms part of a general strategy of destabilization and defamiliarization operative in the film. Those street views mentioned by Taubin are a case in point. A Torontonian might recognize some of this street-level footage, but the most disorienting aspect of this B-roll footage is the way it is integrated into the film's mise-en-scène. As Caetlin Benson-Allott observes, "there are noticeable disjunctions between the interior and exterior components of [the limousine shots] that denaturalize the limo's relation to the world 'around' it."[17] She cites in this regard lead compositor James Cooper's remark that Cronenberg "did not want the cityscape outside to feel too real."[18] In order to accomplish this unnatural effect, Cooper and his team imperfectly matched the B-roll footage with the camera angles inside the limo, and they gave the background plates "the dusky appearance of rear projection screens by making the 'natural' light coming into the limo brighter than the 'natural' light outside."[19] Finally, the movement of these street views past the car windows is "implausibly smooth, as if Packer occupies a New York without potholes or patches."[20] As a result of these effects, Benson-Allott concludes, "Packer visibly does not occupy the same universe as the world outside his limo."[21]

Similarly disorienting is a disequilibrium built into the film's sound design. Packer explains at one point that he had his limousine "Prousted," a reference to Marcel Proust, the French modernist writer who had the walls of his apartment lined with cork in order to mute the sounds of Paris streets. This explanation accounts for the low level of street noise in the limo scenes. However, it does not explain the near absence of ambient noises during the scenes in the first part of the film where Packer steps out of the car and into the outside world. In the restaurant scene evoked above, for example, prior to the arrival of the rat-bearing protestors, Elise and Eric sit at the lunch counter of a crowded Midtown restaurant. Anyone who has had a dining experience of this sort can attest to the high level of noise in a busy establishment like this one. In Cronenberg's film, we hear almost nothing of the conversations happening around the couple. We see the discussions taking place, but they remain conspicuously inaudible. It is as if Packer's entire world—indeed, the entire first act of the film—were "Prousted." If, as Benson-Allott argues in relation to the image track, "Packer visibly does not occupy the same universe as the world outside his limo," he audibly does not belong to that world either. The sound track accomplishes in this way an alienating effect akin to the disorienting visual effects produced on the screen: an effect that not only enables us to appreciate Packer's alienation from the world around him, but which simultaneously alienates us.

These audio and visual effects of defamiliarization and disorientation find a different sort of expression in the movie's dialog, which bears little resemblance to that of a mainstream narrative film. Virtually all of the conversations in the film are characterized by non-sequiturs and ellipses. Characters talk past one another rather than to each other, speaking in short and choppy sentences that often have little bearing on either the preceding sentences or the ones that follow.

Much of this dialog is copied verbatim from DeLillo's novel, which reads like an extended prose poem. However, the phenomenological experience of reading words on the page is of a different order than the experience one has of an audio-visual document that unfolds in real time. One might or might not visualize the scene while reading, imagining (or not) how the characters might look and sound as they move through an imaginary narrative space. The reader might skim or skip certain passages, scrutinize or reread others, and perpetually adjust the pace of reading without necessarily making a conscious decision to do so. In a film, by contrast, the sights and sounds and the pacing of the scenes are fixed. Actors incarnate the roles, deliver the lines with intonations and cadences that take a definitive form in the final cut, and exist in audible-visible spaces for determinate lengths of time.

These differences between the two media make watching Cronenberg's film a stranger and more uncanny experience than reading DeLillo's book. DeLillo's arcane prose allows us to perceive the characters as abstractions in ways that the physical presence on the screen of Packer and his associates does not. As a result, Cronenberg's *Cosmopolis* has a capacity to unsettle the viewer more effectively (or, in any case, differently) than DeLillo's book does the reader. Reading *Cosmopolis*, one may well sense that Packer and company are strange creatures living in an alien world. Watching the film, we cannot help feeling simultaneously that we too are aliens in a strange world. In order to show Packer's disconnection from his surroundings, Cronenberg disconnects us from the film world.

The subtle and not-so-subtle distortions of geographical space and urban sounds enumerated above contribute to this experience of estrangement. So too does the movie's cryptic dialog. Indeed, one of the most disconcerting features of Cronenberg's film stems from his decision to retain DeLillo's abstruse prose more or less intact. Let us take an example.

Roughly 50 minutes into the film, Eric spies his newlywed wife, Elise, smoking a cigarette beneath a theater marquee. He steps out of the limousine and greets her, the two of them chat for a minute, and he invites her to dinner. The scene then cuts to a shot of the newlyweds sitting in an otherwise empty high-class restaurant. The scene starts *in medias res*:

> ERIC: You're wearing a *peau de soie* cocktail dress.
> ELISE: Yes.
> ERIC: It's navy blue.
> ELISE: Yes.
> ERIC: And that's your silver Lucite jewelry.
> ELISE: Yes, it is.
> ERIC: I'm noticing. How was the play?
> ELISE: I left at intermission, didn't I?
> ERIC: What was it about and who was in it? I'm making conversation.

In his commentary on this exchange, Boyle points out a change in register between Packer's two self-referential statements. When Packer says, "I'm noticing," in reference to his observations about Elise's clothes and jewelry, he is playing the part of a husband taking an interest in his wife. But when he says, "I'm making conversation"—and even more explicitly when he later tells her "This is good. We're like people talking. Isn't this how they talk?"—"we are reminded," Boyle comments, "not to mistake him for a human being, let alone a husband."[22] The analysis rings true. However, at the same time, these self-reflexive observations simultaneously provide an implicit meta-commentary on what conversation is. Packer undoubtedly does come across here, as elsewhere, like a human simulacrum, but to the extent that we too may feel at times that, in our daily conversations, we are "like people talking," imitating the way that human beings are supposed to interact, his remarks here on the art of conversation — and more generally, his failed attempts to make human contact throughout the film — uncannily (and uncomfortably) reflect back to us the artificiality and awkwardness of our own social interactions.

Essential to this double estrangement, which I will momentarily relate to what Bertolt Brecht calls the *Verfremdungseffekt*, are the actors' performances. Numerous film critics panned the film for its inability to create believable three-dimensional characters with which audience members could identify. Film critic Roger Moore typifies this sentiment when he writes that "there's no heat to [Pattinson's] performance." The same reviewer, once again giving voice to a common criticism of the film, likewise observes that Sarah Gadon's Elise "is emotionally barren and such a perfectly gorgeous specimen you'd swear she's a cyborg. Like Eric."[23] It is hard to argue with these assessments of Gadon's and Pattinson's interpretations of their roles. These actors' expressionless performances have the effect of reducing their characters to two-dimensional cardboard cutouts. The performers deliver their lines as if on a first read-through of the script.

However, this assessment of the actors' performances need not be taken as a criticism. Indeed, they follow some of the key prescriptions that playwright and stage director Bertolt Brecht makes to the actor in his writings on the theater. In his admiring remarks on Peter Lorre's performance in *Mann ist Mann*, for example, Brecht lauds the actor for creating the impression of "a man simply reading" the dialog "without understanding what it meant."[24] Writing in praise of Helene Weigel's interpretation of the title character in *Die Mutter*, he celebrates the way Weigel "spoke sentences as if they were in the third person," distancing herself from her character to such an extent that her lines were spoken as if by a detached commentator.[25] Such techniques of distanciation, which insert a gap between the actor and the role she plays, are meant to produce a correlative gap between the spectator and the dramatis personae on the stage. As Brecht writes in his famous essay on Chinese acting techniques, the actor should play her part "in such a way that the audience [is] hindered from simply identifying itself with the characters in the play."[26] "The performer's self-observation, an artful and artistic act of self-alienation," he writes of the Chinese actor, "stopped the spectator from losing himself in the character completely."[27] Although Gadon and Pattinson may have had neither these techniques nor their intended effects in mind on the set of *Cosmopolis*, their acting styles and the effects that they produce bear more than a little resemblance to those advocated by Brecht.

In his book on Brecht and method, Fredric Jameson helpfully distinguishes four different valences that the term *Verfremdung* ("alienation" or "estrangement") receives in Brecht's writings, all of which are applicable to Cronenberg's film. Sometimes the *Verfremdungseffekt*, as Brecht calls it (a term generally translated as "alienation effect" or "distancing effect," although Jameson opts for the more neutral "V-effect" along the model of Brecht's abbreviation of the slogan to *V-effekt*), "is evoked in terms of the effect itself that names it."[28] This acceptation of the word, Jameson comments, which involves making the familiar look strange, is the one associated with the Russian formalists, whose techniques of *ostranenie* or "defamiliarization" strove to make us look at the world "with new eyes," breaking us out of our habitual ways of seeing, counteracting our "perceptual numbness," and enabling us to see the world afresh.[29]

A second modality of *Verfremdung*, very different from the first, entails revealing the everyday acts of mimicry in which we engage on a daily basis. Whereas the first sense "implies the antecedence of a general familiarity," this second understanding of the term aims to render perceptible the inherent artificiality of social interactions.[30] In this purview, Jameson writes that the Brechtian theater "should try to demonstrate to the audience that we are all actors, and that acting is an inescapable dimension of social and everyday life."[31] For Brecht, "everybody always acts," asserts Jameson.[32] A quintessential "Brechtian" character in this sense, for Jameson, is Jean-Paul Sartre's waiter who "plays at being a waiter."[33] This tragic-comic figure, who makes his memorable appearance in chapter 2 of *Being and Nothingness*, "not only illustrates a theory of being, or of the lack of being, he also dramatizes a whole dramaturgy."[34]

These two types of estrangement appear in various guises in *Cosmopolis*. The first type is particularly apparent in the distortions of physical-geographical space and the urban soundscape. The dialog and the actors' performances also "defamiliarize" social life, enabling us to see human interactions in a new light, stripped of their naturalist veneer. Brecht could almost be talking about a film like *Cosmopolis* when he writes, in his "Short Description of a New Technique of Acting which Produces an Alienation Effect," "Characters and incidents from ordinary life, from our immediate surroundings, being familiar, strike us as more or less natural. Alienating them helps make them remarkable to us."[35]

Yet the non-naturalistic dialog in *Cosmopolis* also produces a V-effect in the second sense enumerated by Jameson. During the dinner scene alluded to above, for example, when Eric tells Elise, "I'm making conversation," or when he says to her, "We're like people talking," he draws attention to the fact that he is an affect alien posing as a human being. This is Boyle's interpretation of the scene. Yet we may also hear in his remarks a more general commentary on social interactions. In the first instance, we see Eric as an impostor; in the second, we perceive human behavior itself as imposture. The acting styles of Gadon and Pattinson reinforce these two different alienation effects. On the one hand, the actors' unconvincing performances make their characters seem like automata impersonating human beings; on the other hand, Gadon's and Pattinson's detached readings of the lines simultaneously convey the extent to which conversations in the real world approximate exchanges between automata. From the first perspective, we have the impression of robots impersonating people; from the second, of people imitating robots.

Brecht's recommended acting techniques and his dramaturgy more generally—which includes innovations in set design and the insertion of "intertitles" between scenes and of songs within scenes—aim to prevent the spectator from losing herself in the story. The episodic structure of the film's first hour, a structure which interrupts the movie's narrative flow and inhibits the spectator's ability to get carried away by the drama, serves a similar purpose in *Cosmopolis*. With little effort, one could imagine giving Brecht-like chapter titles to the limo scenes ("Chapter 1, in which Eric Packer, Chief Executive Officer of Packer Capital, wants a haircut"; "Chapter 2, in which Shiner assures Packer that their system is secure"; and so forth).

The twin foils against which Brecht directs his polemic here are the Aristotelian notion of catharsis and Konstatin Stanislavski's influential method of acting. Both Stanislavski's acting method (known simply as "the method"), which requires the actor to enter into the skin of the character and essentially "become" her for the performance, and Aristotle's theory of catharsis, a purging of emotions of pity and fear, are affairs of identification: in the first case, of the actor with her role; in the second, of the spectator with the character. The former of these two identifications can be seen as a means to achieving the latter.

The more authentically the performer plays the role, the more emotionally involved the spectator can become and as a result, the more intense the cathartic response to the work may be. In order to appreciate the extent to which *Cosmopolis* does not use these means to achieve this sort of end, we might conduct a thought experiment and imagine what the film would be like if contemporary method actors such as Leonardo DiCaprio and Cate Blanchett played Eric and Elise. Instead of the dispassionate and alienating performances of Pattinson and Gadon, we would risk getting impassioned and engrossing performances like those delivered by DiCaprio in *The Wolf of Wall Street* (2013) and Blanchett in *Blue Jasmine* (2013).

These anti-Aristotelian and anti-Stanislavskian polemics, which, Jameson recognizes, allow one "to accuse [Brecht's] theatre of being cold and intellectualistic on the one hand, and propagandistic on the other," constitute Jameson's third way of approaching the V-effect, which he characterizes as "the turning off or shutting down of *Entfühlung*, of empathy or even sympathy."[36] Yet this third modality of estrangement leads to "the fourth and final, ultimately political, formulation of the V-effect, which is meant to subsume all the preceding descriptions, and place them in a new light":

> Here, the familiar or habitual is reidentified as the "natural," and its estrangement reveals that appearance, which suggests the changeless and the eternal as well, and shows the object to be instead "historical," to which may be added, as a political corollary, made or constructed by human beings, and thus able to be changed by them as well, or replaced altogether.[37]

Writing, in this vein, in praise of "the instructive theatre" (meaning his own), Brecht proclaims: "The theatre became an affair for philosophers, but only for such philosophers as wished not just to explain the world but also to change it."[38]

One of Brecht's many paraphrases of Marx's eleventh thesis on Feuerbach, this statement presents the theater as an engaged, materialist practice aimed at transforming the world rather than merely reflecting it. The arsenal of dramaturgical "estrangement" techniques that the playwright proposes, serve this openly political aim, in Jameson's estimation, by showing the natural and seemingly immutable world to be cultural and historical, and therefore subject to change.

In its own way, Cronenberg's *Cosmopolis* also shows the world to be a malleable construction. Within the mise-en-scène, for example, the cityscape that rolls past the limo's windows "in the form of intentionally fake-looking rear projections" suggests the artificiality and plasticity of the world.[39] Meanwhile, the off-kilter dialog and the actors' stilted delivery of their lines serve to remind us that we too are "constructions" and that we too are subject to change. This idea that people can change might sound like a self-evident truism, but it runs counter to one of the fundamental ideologies of Hollywood cinema, which by and large presents characters as immutable "types" that maintain their identity in the face of whatever challenges they may confront. Finally, on the allegorical level of the plot, the movie suggests that capitalism, which has taken on the appearance of an inevitable fact in the present age, is neither fixed nor permanent. It too is a human construction, the film reminds us; it too can be changed or "replaced altogether."

Leveraging Fictitious Capital

The film's second part, which begins when Packer arrives at his family barbershop and ends with the tycoon submitting to his execution-style murder, plunges us into a different world than the synthetic techno-space of the first act. Shot on realistic sets with rich mises-en-scène, they take place in believable settings unlike the surrealistic virtual world created for the limo scenes. The dilapidated spaces of an old-time barbershop, seemingly unchanged for generations save half a century of wear and decay, and the decrepit warehouse where Richard Sheets has taken up residence, stand in sharp contrast to the slick interior of Packer's limousine. The string of smart and generally young consultants, advisers, and associates that enter the limo to meet with Eric belong to a different social milieu than the working-class octogenarian that cuts Packer's hair and the unemployed, unbathed, and uncouth Sheets that Eric confronts at the end of the film. Moreover, Paul Giamatti's interpretation of the destitute Sheets conveys a psychological depth and a pathos lacking in the two-dimensional cardboard cutouts that populate the first act. Additionally, the viewer experiences none of the temporal or spatial dislocations that characterize the first hour of the film. Even the editing seems more motivated in the second act. Aesthetically and dramatically, the last 30 or so minutes of *Cosmopolis* seem to belong to a different movie than the first hour. Ideologically, however, the two segments belong together. Depicting the contrasting yet complementary faces of twenty-first-century capitalism, they present the recto and verso of contemporary neoliberalism.

As Thomas Piketty's monumental book on capital in the twenty-first century demonstrates, wealth inequality is currently at its highest level since the Great Crash of 1929.[40] In contrast to the reduction of class differences that took place following the Great Depression, however, when wealth inequality reached its lowest level in recorded economic history, the trend following the Great Recession of the twenty-first century has been (following a dip in 2009) in the direction of ever-more extreme inequality. If we continue on our current trajectory, the gap between the wealthiest people in the world and the rest of the world's population will soon be wider than it has ever been. Already, Piketty reports, the United States has "a record level of inequality of income from labor (probably higher than in any other society at any time in the past, anywhere in the world)."[41]

One of the driving forces behind this increasingly inequitable distribution of wealth is the growth of finance capital. As David Harvey shows in *A Brief History of Neoliberalism*, the deregulation of the financial sector that began in the 1980s "allowed the financial system to become one of the main centres of redistributive activity."[42] "Increasingly freed from the regulatory constraints and barriers that had hitherto confined its field of action," Harvey writes, "financial activity could flourish as never before."[43] Not coincidentally, Harvey's graph, in *The Enigma of Capital*, of the rise of the US financial sector from the early 1980s, when it accounted for roughly 15 percent of domestic corporate profits, to the mid-2000s, by which time it had come to represent 45 percent of those profits, follows virtually the same pattern as Piketty's graph of the growth of wealth inequality in the country over the same time period.[44] Superimposing one chart onto the other, one would barely be able to distinguish the two lines.

This role that finance capital has played in exacerbating wealth inequalities has obvious relevance to Cronenberg's story of a super-rich asset manager's death at the hands of a dejected former employee. The particular commodity that Packer trades, and the means by which he trades it, are also significant. Let us examine them each in turn.

As Marx explains in volume 3 of *Capital*, the commodities bought and sold on the stock market represent, in the first instance, real capital invested in manufacturing. Yet at the same time, he points out, company stock simultaneously replicates that real capital, essentially doubling it and reproducing it in a spectral form. A shoe company, for instance, might own, say, a billion dollars' worth of shoes, raw materials, machinery, real estate, and so forth. Meanwhile, the company stock, which is bought and sold on a market separate from the one where people buy and sell shoes, may also be worth a billion dollars. From a billion dollars' worth of raw materials, inventory, and infrastructure, one suddenly magically has 2 billion dollars. Moreover, Marx observes, the value of those company shares—those "nominal representatives of non-existent capitals," as he calls them—"can rise and fall quite independently of the movement in value of the actual capital to which they are titles."[45] While the shoe company might own assets worth a billion dollars, its value on the stock market might rise to double, triple, or quadruple that amount, or it might plummet to next to nothing.

Currency exchange, then, Packer's particular area of specialization, trades in a doubly fictitious form of capital. A further step removed from production, it deals with the buying and selling of universal representatives of value, including the value of those nominal representatives of the capital that Marx calls "real." Since Richard Nixon eliminated the gold standard and "floated" the dollar in 1971, national and regional currencies have become bona fide commodities in their own right, subject to market forces irreducible to those affecting other sectors of the economy. Financiers like George Soros have made billions in this market. His notorious shorting of the British pound in 1992, when he bet against the United Kingdom's ability to stay within the European Exchange Rate Mechanism, netted him $10 billion in one trade.

Part of what has made currency trading—in fact, all speculative trade in regulated (as well as many unregulated) markets—so profitable in recent decades is companies' ability to leverage large sums of money. Whereas, according to Harvey, investment banks typically leverage up to three times the value of their cash on hand, "by 2005 the leveraging rate went up as high as 30 to 1. No wonder," Harvey wryly comments, "the world appeared to be awash with surplus liquidity" in the 2000s. It was flooded with "surplus fictitious capital."[46] It goes without saying that this increased leverage also exposes firms to increased risk. Although we do not know how leveraged Packer Capital is in *Cosmopolis*, we do know that it is enough to decimate the company. Following the path that led Lehman

Brothers into the abyss in 2008—a path followed by every major Wall Street bank and that would have annihilated every one of them if the taxpayers had not bailed them out—Packer makes high-stakes bets with money he does not have. When it turns out that he lost his gamble on the yuan, he therefore suddenly finds himself in freefall.

Alienated Labor and Global Immiseration

At the opposite side of the social spectrum from the high-rolling Eric Packer is Richard Sheets. Nearly every salient aspect of these two figures sets them apart. Pattinson's and Giamatti's contrasting physical appearances, for example, are exaggerated by Sheets' artless comb-over, the ratty towel he alternately wears over his shoulders and on his head, and the glistening sweat that covers his body. In regards to acting, while Pattinson underplays his role to the point of being a cipher, Giamatti invests his character with passion and pathos. The adjective that comes to mind to describe Giamatti's performance is *embodied*, a word one would not readily apply to Pattinson's interpretation of Packer. Sheets is almost excessively corporal. We can practically smell his body odor emanating from the screen.

The native spaces that the two characters inhabit reinforce the opposition between the two figures. The state-of-the-art luxury limousine of the first act, with its shiny leather seats, glowing computer screens, and gleaming glass side tables, bespeaks the prosperity of its owner. Sheets' desolate squat, by contrast, is strewn with obsolete technology and discarded office supplies. Heaps of adding machines, outdated PCs, metal lamps, and dusty manila folders filled with who-knows-what documents sit piled up on stainless steel desks and filing cabinets. Whereas the electric blue graphs and charts that radiate from the computer screens of Packer's limo look futuristic, Sheets' squat is a graveyard for the unwanted refuse of offices past.

As Marxist cultural critics like Jameson, Alberto Toscano,

and Jeff Kinkle have shown, capital as such is notoriously difficult to represent.[47] The dynamic graphs and charts on the computer monitors in Packer's limo can be perceived as one attempt to visualize it. Indeed, the limousine's interior in and of itself comes across like a cinematic attempt to give concrete visual form to an abstraction that eludes direct depiction. The opulent high-tech interior of the Packer mobile connotes not only wealth but also the mechanisms and processes of capitalist accumulation. Conversely and correlatively, Sheets' makeshift residence, cluttered with the rejectamenta of a postindustrial society, represents the other side of this economic process. The trash strewn around Sheets' squat conjures bygone industries and obsolescent modes of production. Whereas Packer's limousine evokes the mobile capital of the twenty-first century, the crumbling warehouse where Sheets has taken up residence connotes a bygone era of fixed capital. *Cosmopolis* helps us see the decline of the latter mode of production as a consequence of the rise of the former regime of accumulation. Sheets' miserable conditions of existence are a direct byproduct of Packer's means of wealth extraction. The lamentable squat that Sheets calls home and Packer's immaculate limo represent two sides of the same process. One is the recto to the other's verso.

The centerpiece of Sheets' squat is the squatter himself, a hollow shell of a man as obsolete and redundant as the useless clutter that surrounds him. In his analysis of the film's final sequence, Boyle aptly argues that this piece of human offal "symbolizes what Marx calls the 'relative surplus population.'"[48] Referencing Jameson's timely proposition, in *Representing Capital*, that Marx's *Capital* is first and foremost "a book about unemployment,"[49] Boyle remarks: "Instead of representing a specific social class, Sheets epitomizes the precarity and potential immiseration of all laborers. He embodies the universality of the system precisely because he is excluded from it."[50] This interpretation serves as an apposite reminder of the fate of human labor in the global economy. As Harvey observes in *Seventeen Contradictions and the End of Capitalism*, "Most of the world's population is becoming disposable and irrelevant from the standpoint of capital."[51] Putting concrete numbers to this state of affairs, Slavoj Žižek predicts that "the coming global economy will tend towards a state in which only 20 percent of the labor force are able to do all the necessary work, so that 80 percent of people will be basically irrelevant and of no use, thus potentially unemployed."[52] This scenario lends urgency to the fourth modality of estrangement operative in Cronenberg's film: the reminder that capitalism is (in Jameson's words) "made or constructed by human beings, and thus able to be changed by them as well, or replaced altogether." The implicit response to the rhetorical question that Žižek asks in regards to the bleak scenario he describes above—"is not a system which renders 80 percent of people irrelevant and useless *itself irrelevant and of no use?*"—is a clear and emphatic "yes."[53]

Sheets is emblematic of the fate of human labor under capitalism in a second way as well. Before being laid off and joining the growing ranks of the unemployed, he worked for Packer as a currency analyst specializing in the Thai baht. "I loved the baht!" he tells Packer during their confrontation in the film's last scene. "But your system is so micro-timed that I couldn't keep up with it. I couldn't find it. It is so infinitesimal. I began to hate my work, and you, and all the numbers on my screen, and every minute of my life." If this is not an illustration of the phenomenon that Marx called "alienated labor," I don't know what is. Granted, Marx had in mind principally the alienation of manual laborers in the factory, who suffer the double alienation of being estranged from the products of their labor and from themselves in the act of producing, and thereby from what Marx calls their "species-being."[54] However, as Erich Fromm argued more than half a century ago, "If anything, the clerk, the salesman, the executive, are even more alienated today than the skilled manual worker."[55] The recent introduction of metrics and assessment tools designed to measure the productivity of immaterial labor even in such sectors as higher education follows a general logic of labor alienation. Such metrics, nowhere more codified than in the United Kingdom, risk turning what could potentially be such gratifying work as academic research into alienated labor.

"Working is not just the creation of economic wealth," André Gorz writes in the *Critique of Economic Reason*; "it is also always a means of self-creation."[56] In this context, the recent Gallop pole, cited by Harvey, showing that "about 70 per cent of full-time workers either hated going to work or had mentally checked out," speaks volumes about the selves we have created under the current conditions of capitalism.[57] In sum, it is not just the unfortunate 80 percent of the population that the system throws out of work who suffer the ill effects of neoliberalism. If merely 30 percent of the small percentage of people lucky enough to find full-time employment derive pleasure from the work that they do, we are left with a tiny minority of people for whom the system is working. The hapless Sheets represents the other 95 percent of the population. When, in his admittedly deranged state, he decides to murder the person he deems responsible for his misery, he acts for us all.

Chapter 3

The Rationality of Revolt: *Suffragette*

The UK theatrical release poster for *Suffragette*, Sarah Gavron's 2015 film about a group of working-class women in London's East End who fought the British government for women's right to vote at the beginning of the twentieth century, shows actresses Carey Mulligan, Helena Bonham Carter, and Meryl Streep in period dress standing shoulder to shoulder against a purple, white, and green banner. Superimposed in block letters over the three figures appear the words: "The time is now." This tagline is curious. As most filmgoers would know, women have had the right to vote in the United Kingdom for nearly a century. Certain women in Britain gained "the franchise," as it was called at the time, in 1918, and electoral equality with men was achieved a decade later, in 1928. The film is set during the years 1912–13, when the suffragettes escalated their militant tactics by embarking on a campaign of vandalism and sabotage in conjunction with their ongoing political activities. Gavron and screenwriter Abi Morgan conducted extensive research in drafting their story, and they went to great lengths to create the look and feel of London at the beginning of the twentieth century.[1] The movie is, in sum, a carefully constructed piece of historical fiction firmly rooted in pre-World War I Britain. Yet the movie poster asserts that "the time is now." What are we to make of this suggestion that this film about a bygone era, depicting a battle that was waged roughly a century ago, pertains to the present?

The movie's tagline is undoubtedly a publicity strategy designed to make this historical drama about a long-past era seem relevant in today's world. The phrase comes across as preemptive counter spin, urging moviegoers that might not care too much about events that took place over a century ago, or who may not care for period dramas, that the events depicted in the movie remain current more than 100 years after they occurred. Yet these events do remain current. *Suffragette* is an eminently timely film. It raises issues that remain pertinent in twenty-first-century Britain and advanced capitalist democracies more generally, while urging us to consider the current working conditions of millions of people, especially women, in the developing world. However, beyond conjuring images of exploitation and oppression that remain current in the "post-feminist" era of global neoliberalism, what *Suffragette* offers is, above all, a timely reminder of how social progress has been achieved in the past. Faced with a democratically elected government that seems impervious to their demands, the working-class women in *Suffragette* offer us a way past our current political impasse in so-called democratic states. While the preceding chapters offer numerous reasons why progressives living in parliamentary democracies may feel compelled to revolt at the beginning of the twenty-first century, *Suffragette* suggests a hypothetical scenario of how to do so. By returning to the past, Gavron indicates a possible way to move forward.

This chapter examines the hypothetical path forward that the movie proposes to the viewer. Following a plot summary, it first considers salient differences between Gavron's story and canonical histories of the militant women's suffrage movement in Britain, pondering the resonances of the filmmaker's version of events in the current sociopolitical context. One of the most obvious differences between Gavron's story and mainstream accounts of British suffragism stems from the filmmaker's decision to center her story on a group of working-class women as opposed to the more famous upper-class women in the movement. This decision enables the filmmaker to embed a narrative of class oppression and class struggle within the story of the Votes for Women campaign in Edwardian England. The resulting intermeshing of narratives of class antagonism and the fight for women's enfranchisement has far-reaching implications in the early twenty-first century. In the current context—a context in which waning working-class consciousness and rising levels of exploitation and domination by an international capitalist class go hand in hand—it is undoubtedly the narrative of class antagonism that is the more controversial of the two. Even the most vociferous antifeminists in contemporary Britain would not seriously propose returning to an archaic conception of political entitlement that would disenfranchise half of the adult population in one fell swoop.

At the turn of the twentieth century, by contrast, the idea that women might enjoy the same political rights as men was the subject of much mockery, even among women. Alice Guy-Blaché's *The Consequences of Feminism* (1906), for example—made by the world's first female filmmaker and arguably the first director of a fiction film (*The Cabbage Fairy*, 1896)—shows women in porkpie hats dominating feminized men, whose roles have been reduced, in the film, to ironing clothes, looking after the children, dressing up in frilly hats, gossiping among themselves, and fending off advances from sexually assertive women. The film does not present this reversal of traditional gender roles as something to celebrate but, on the contrary, something to scorn. The "consequence of feminism" evoked in the movie's title is the breakdown of the social structure that the advocates for women's rights were bringing about by "acting like men." There was nothing original about this idea at the time. It was depicted on picture postcards, illustrated in newspaper cartoons and on posters, and proffered regularly on the floor of the House of Commons in the early years of the twentieth century.[2]

The fact that *Suffragette* is the first and, to date, the only film in the history of cinema that the British government has allowed to be filmed on location inside the House of Commons is indicative of how uncontroversial women's suffrage has become since the days of Alice Guy-Blaché.[3] The inherently divisive notion of social class, by contrast, has become so unfashionable in the neoliberal period that it has almost become anachronistic. By casting the Votes for Women campaign as a working-class movement, Gavron revives the old-fashioned idea of class warfare while recounting the story of the women's fight for the vote. In so doing, she effectively smuggles in a controversial idea under the guise of a now widely accepted one. The implication is that if the suffragettes' ends justified their means 100 years ago, similar acts of civil disobedience would be justified today if people lived under similar conditions. One need only make the connection between the working-class women in *Suffragette* and their contemporary counterparts for this interpretation to impose itself upon the viewer.

Following a series of comparisons between the women's situation in *Suffragette* and the conditions of contemporary women in both the developed world and the developing world, the chapter then examines the two principal forms of contestation that the Votes for Women campaign takes in the film. The first of these two forms of agitation appears in condensed form in the movie's one-word title. In contrast to the suffra*gists*, who "campaigned for votes for women constitutionally i.e. within the law," the suffra*gettes* campaigned for votes for women by "adopting militant tactics i.e. involving breaking the law."[4] As feminist theorist Simone de Beauvoir shows in her 1949 account of women's suffrage campaigns around the world, the British suffragettes' recourse to violence is historically unique among women's suffrage movements. Nowhere else in the world did the fight for votes for women take the openly confrontational and decisively violent turn that it did in Britain. "Around 1903," Beauvoir recounts, "feminist claims took a singular turn. In London, the Pankhurst family created the Women's Social and Political Union, which joined with the Labour Party and embarked on resolutely militant activities."[5] Beauvoir details the numerous forms of engagement in which the Women's Social and Political Union (WSPU) took part. Led primarily by Emmeline Pankhurst and her daughter Christabel, the WSPU organized mass rallies in Hyde Park and Trafalgar Square, marched on the Albert Hall during Liberal Party meetings, sent delegation after delegation to Parliament to plead the women's cause, and picketed outside the House of Commons to protest the government's inaction. Militant suffragettes forced their way into the Prime Minister's office and chained themselves to the railing of his residence at 10 Downing Street; they insulted and spat at the police, were subject to mass arrests for their actions, and adopted hunger-strike tactics while in jail. In 1910, a 6-mile-long column marched through London in anticipation of the government's response to a proposed suffrage bill. When the motion failed to pass the Chamber, the suffragettes escalated their militant campaign. "In 1912," Beauvoir recounts, "they adopted a more violent tactic: they burned empty houses, slashed pictures, trampled flower beds, threw stones at the police."[6] The filmmakers, who situate the film action in the climactic years of 1912 and 1913, subtly conjure this rich and controversial history in their one-word title. "Suffragette" (a term never adopted by suffrage activists in the United States) refers to a particularly militant group of women in a specific country at a particular moment in history.

Beyond their willingness to resort to violence in order to further their cause, the second characteristic of the women's engagement in *Suffragette* is a presupposition of equality on their part. Based on the assumption that they are men's equals, they demonstrate that they are indeed equal to men and insist that they should therefore have equal rights. In so doing, the movie's protagonists enact a "scene of dissensus," as contemporary philosopher and political theorist Jacques Rancière calls such demonstrations of equality. Rather than basing their campaign on an essentialist (or even a dynamic) conception of collective identity, what the East End suffragettes do is collectively lay claim to a political existence that the British government has denied them. In short, they act like political subjects, thereby forcibly inserting themselves into a political arena in which they had no place. Moving from Rancière's analysis of French feminist Olympe de Gouges' demonstration that she (according to Rancière's interpretation) in fact had the rights that she did not have and yet did not have the rights that she nonetheless had, to his analogous interpretation of a workers' strike in nineteenth-century France, I conclude with an exploration of the ways in which Rancière's conception of political subjectivization helps us interpret the women's actions in the film, and how it might help us think about modes of political engagement in the twenty-first century.

The Making of a Suffragette

The narrative strategy that Gavron and Morgan adopt in order to engage the viewer and solicit her complicity is the tried-and-true method of presenting a central character with whom the film encourages us to identify. This character, the bright and genial but uneducated and relatively apolitical Maud Watts (Carey Mulligan), is a worker at the fictional Glasshouse Laundry in the working-class neighborhood of Bethnal Green in the East End of London. Maud lives in a cramped tenement with her husband, Sonny (Ben Whisaw), who also works at the laundry, and their young son, George (Adam Michael Dodd). We learn that Maud has progressed steadily through the ranks at the laundry, where she started working part-time when she was 7 years old and full-time from the age of 12, becoming head washer at 17 and forewoman at 20. The movie alludes to sexual harassment that she has experienced at work at the hands of her supervisor, Mr Taylor (Geoff Bell), but she seems to have adapted to the hostile work environment and, at the outset of the movie, is a trusted and loyal employee.

Maud's political awakening occurs in stages. At the beginning of the film, she witnesses a suffragette window-breaking campaign in London's fashionable West End. She recognizes her coworker Violet Miller (Ann-Marie Duff) among the stone throwers, but Maud's involvement in the incident is purely that of a bystander. The first indication that Maud has any sympathy for the suffragettes occurs when she intervenes on Violet's behalf in order to save her from a tongue-lashing from Taylor. Then, exiting the factory later that day, Maud and her coworkers encounter an upper-class women's suffrage activist by the name of Alice Haughton (Romola Garai), who informs the gathering crowd that the government has agreed to hear testimonies from working women around the country. Alice recruits Violet to represent the Glasshouse Laundry, but on the day she is scheduled to give her testimony, Violet arrives at Parliament with bruises on her face, the result of a beating she received from her husband the night before. Alice then persuades Maud, who has accompanied Violet for moral support, to deliver a testimony in Violet's place. We sense a slow conversion taking place in Maud as she overcomes her initial timidity and begins putting into words the hardships she has suffered as a working woman in the hardscrabble East End. Following her testimony, the Right Honorable David Lloyd George (Adrian Schiller), who presides over the proceedings, thanks Maud for her eloquent testimony and informs her that "an amendment to the [suffrage] bill might just force the change towards the vote." Pleased that her testimony was effective and heartened by Lloyd George's encouraging words, Maud has completed the first stage of her conversion. She has passed from apathy to sympathy and then, however reluctantly, to active involvement.

Maud then starts mingling with the suffragettes. She and Violet become friends, and a certain Edith Ellyn (played by Helena Bonham Carter, who is incidentally the great-granddaughter of Prime Minister HH Asquith, the suffragettes' staunch opponent during the pre-World War I years), a middle-class pharmacist in the East End and a self-proclaimed "soldier" in the suffragette movement, invites Maud to tea and brings her into the fold.

An additional step forward in Maud's political apprenticeship, followed by a full step back, occurs when a crowd of women's suffrage activists gathered on Parliament Square learn from the silver-tongued Lloyd George that, after considerable debate in the House of Commons, "it was carried that there was not the evidence to support any change to the suffrage bill." Maud and her fellow protestors begin yelling at Lloyd George, who rushes off in his motorcar as police move in to disperse the crowd. The ensuing clash between the women and the police results in countless demonstrators, including Maud, being carted away to Holloway prison. Upon her release from Holloway a week or so later, Maud returns home to Sonny, who is furious with her. He explains that the police came around to talk to him, that the neighbors are gossiping, and that everyone at work knows that she went to jail for a cause for which the vast majority of the people at the laundry, including most of the women, show little sympathy. "You won't ever shame me like that again," Sonny tells Maud, whose downcast eyes signal her acquiescence.

The decisive turning point in Maud's political itinerary occurs a few scenes later, in the course of an unspectacular conversation between her and Sonny. Violet has urged Maud to accompany her to hear Emmeline Pankhurst speak at a rally in Camden Town, in north London. Having promised Sonny that she will cease her involvement with the suffragettes, Maud informs Violet that she cannot attend the rally, but then a few days later, lying in bed on the morning of the Camden rally, she asks her husband what kind of life their daughter would have if they had had a girl instead of a boy. "Same as yours," Sonny replies, as if the answer was obvious. A close-up on Maud's face as she stares off into the distance, then tells Sonny that she will be "working late" that night, subtly indicates a decision silently made.

The rest of the film depicts Maud's deepening engagement with the suffragettes. She attends the rally at Camden Square, where Mrs Pankhurst (Meryl Streep) addresses a large crowd from the balcony of a house overlooking the square: "Be militant, each of you in your own way," the orator exhorts the crowd. "Those of you who can break windows, break them. Those of you who can further attack the sacred idol of property, do so. We have been left with no alternative but to defy this government. [...] I incite this meeting, and all the women in Britain, to rebellion!" she enjoins the assembly, before delivering her famous parting remark: "I would rather be a rebel than a slave!"

As Mrs Pankhurst delivers her closing line, the police arrive and break up the meeting. In contrast to the dispersal of the crowd gathered at Parliament Square earlier in the film, this time Inspector Steed (Brendan Gleeson) instructs the officers not to arrest the women but to drop them at their homes and "let their husbands deal with them." Sonny "deals with" Maud by throwing her and a few armfuls of her belongings out into the street. He forbids Maud to have any more contact with George (which he can do because the law gives him sole custody over the child) and then, unable to care for the boy on his own, he gives him up for adoption. One of the film's most poignant scenes is the parting of Maud and George, when Sonny ships off the young boy to live with a respectable-looking bourgeois couple that boasts of having a house "with a garden."

Without a home, Maud finds refuge in a one-room flat that the WSPU rents for her. She continues working at the laundry in an atmosphere of suspicion and heightened hostility until her boss, the odious Mr Taylor, informs her—while leaning into her and breathing in her ear as he simultaneously tells her of his budding infatuation with a 12-year-old girl at the factory—that he wants her gone. Maud responds by picking up a scalding iron and slamming it down on Taylor's hand, much to the viewer's satisfaction. Arrested again but then released by

Steed, who actually shows a fair amount of sympathy for her, Maud then dedicates herself wholeheartedly to the cause. She and Violet take part in a coordinated campaign to cripple the country's communication network by blowing up letterboxes. She also participates, along with Edith, Emily Wilding Davison (Natalie Press), and Edith's husband, Hugh (Finbar Lynch), in the bombing of Lloyd George's vacant summerhouse. Caught yet again by the police, she is sent once again to Holloway, where prison officials break her hunger strike by pouring milk into a funnel and through a rubber hose inserted deep into her nose. Steed, who observes the force-feeding through the bars of Maud's cell, is visibly shaken by the scene but does not intervene.

The film resolves the building narrative tensions with a fictionalized account of a famous historical incident. Maud, Edith, and Emily Wilding Davison (two fictional characters and a historical figure), frustrated at the dearth of press coverage dedicated to the destruction of Lloyd George's summerhouse, disheartened by a police raid on the WSPU office that left the place a shambles, demoralized by the arrest of several key members of the organization, and desperate to find a way to capture the headlines, come up with the idea of attending the Epsom Derby, a nationally publicized annual horse race, with the aim of taking their cause directly to the king. "We'll raise our flag in front of the world's cameras," Edith proclaims. Fearing that his wife's heart will not withstand another prison sentence, Hugh locks Edith in a back room of the pharmacy in order to prevent her from accompanying her colleagues to the derby, leaving Maud and Emily to carry out the mission on their own. The two suffragettes make their way through the crowd at Epsom Downs but are unable to approach the king. Unwilling to let the mission fail, Emily slips under the fence and runs out into the pitch, weaving in and out of the galloping horses, with a Votes for Women sash in her hand. In a series of shots inspired by famous archival footage of the incident, the climactic scene shows the king's horse, unable to avoid the woman in its path, mowing Emily down and killing her.[7] The movie's last scene dissolves from a fictional reconstruction of Emily Wilding Davison's massive funeral parade through the streets of London in 1913 to newly discovered archival footage of the actual parade. This final film image is followed by a set of intertitles explaining that Wilding Davison's death drew global attention to the suffragettes' cause, noting that some women in Britain gained the ballot in 1918 and that others obtained the franchise in 1928. The film then presents a list, sorted by date, of countries where women achieved the same voting rights as men, from New Zealand, which gave women the vote in 1893, to Saudi Arabia, where in 2015 women were promised voting rights.

Suffragette and the History of the Militant Women's Suffrage Movement in Britain

This film narrative is a mixture of fact and fiction, intertwining actual events and historical figures with fictional characters and hypothetical situations. Emmeline Pankhurst, Emily Wilding Davison, and David Lloyd George are historical figures, for example, whereas Maud, Edith, and Violet are composite characters based on different suffragettes' testimonies.[8] Some of the decisions that the filmmakers make in telling the story of the militant suffrage movement serve the function of streamlining the narrative or condensing the timeline, but others are clearly motivated by ideological, rather than narrative, considerations. The latter are particularly instructive. Let us take a moment to explore some of the salient changes that the filmmakers make to the historical material, and to consider how those changes resonate in the socio-cultural and political context of the early twenty-first century.

The film subjects even the generally known historical events to a process of creative fictionalization. For example, the window-breaking campaign at the beginning of the movie evokes the suffragette raid of March 1, 1912, when "bands of women paraded Regent Street, Piccadilly, the Strand, Oxford Street, and Bond Street, smashing windows with stones and hammers."[9] Yet the riot in front of Parliament, which follows the window-smashing campaign in the movie, clearly alludes to the incident known as Black Friday, which took place in November 1910, nearly a year and a half before the famous 1912 raid on the West End.[10] In her perspicacious film review, historian Linda Gordon calls attention to this reordering of events, which she interprets as a way to give the narrative a clearer shape: "The film reverses the chronology of events, showing the suffragettes' violence first. Although this move obscures the fact that the WSPU was responding to official brutality, it helps build the arc of escalating action."[11] By first presenting the raid on the West End and then showing the police crackdown on the demonstrators in Parliament Square, the filmmakers also create motivation for the government's decision to respond harshly to the assembled women. Gavron and Morgan thereby telescope the chronology, condensing the long-standing antagonism between the suffragettes and government forces into a few short scenes.

Gordon remarks on a second important decision that the filmmakers take regarding the narrative timeline: "Even though concluding the film with Davison's death at the derby leaves us with a woman sacrificing herself, it also avoids a simplistic 'you've-come-a-long-way-baby' happy ending. The truth is that feminism is unfinished."[12] The film reinforces this idea that feminism is an ongoing struggle in the last exchange between Maud and Edith. Handing her colleague a newspaper bearing the headline, "Funeral for Miss Davison. Thousands Expected," Edith tells Maud: "It's in every paper. They say thousands will line the streets." The smile exchanged between the two women, accompanied by a mini-crescendo in the violin composition playing in the background, indicates that this is a moment of triumph for the women's movement. But instead of the facilely saying, "We won," which is what both the imagery and the music suggest, Maud says, more soberly, "We go on."

Ending the story in 1913—a year before the outbreak of the First World War, 5 years before the first woman in Britain cast a ballot, and 15 years before women gained the same voting rights as men—also enables Gavron to sidestep some inconvenient details of the women's rights campaign in Britain. As documentary evidence presented by feminist filmmaker Midge Mackenzie in *Shoulder to Shoulder* makes clear, the British government finally agreed to extend the franchise to women in 1918 largely in recognition of the important role that women played during the war.[13] The intense pressure that suffrage activists put on the government during the years preceding the war surely contributed to furthering the women's cause. It was becoming increasingly difficult to justify the exclusion of women from the political arena in the first decade or so of the twentieth century. But it was the invaluable contributions of women to the war effort that finally forced the government's hand. By ending the film in 1913, following Wilding Davison's death, Gavron enables us to ignore this set of circumstances and to attribute the women's victory principally if not solely to the actions depicted in the film. This decision on the filmmaker's part might blur history a bit, but it makes the film a much more powerful piece of propaganda for the twenty-first-century left.

The decision to conclude the story in 1913 also permits Gavron to downplay the acrimonious divisions within the suffragette movement that occurred at the outbreak of the war and to eschew Emmeline and Christabel Pankhurst's turn to the political right at around that time. In the film, the figure of Emmeline Pankhurst stands in for the leadership of the WSPU, a role that the empirical Mrs Pankhurst shared primarily with her eldest daughter, Christabel, and secondarily with Sylvia Pankhurst, Christabel's younger sister (as well as with a small handful of people outside of the family). Neither Christabel nor Sylvia appears in the film, but the movie does make passing reference to them when Hugh, trying to temper his wife's zeal, tells Edith: "The movement is divided now. Even Sylvia Pankhurst is opposed to her mother and her sister's militant strategy." It is true that Sylvia disagreed with her mother and her sister over the effectiveness, for the movement, of destroying property, but the more radical split within the family occurred along ideological lines, rather than as a result of tactical differences. As Emmeline and Christabel moved further and further to the right, Sylvia moved ever further to the left. It is Sylvia, for example, who, in 1912, organized the women of the East End, campaigning in working-class neighborhoods like Bethnal Green in an effort to recruit working women to the suffragette cause. Christabel, by contrast, did not see the merit in recruiting such an unpromising batch of women. According to Sylvia's account of events, for Christabel, "a working-woman's movement was of no value."[14] In Christabel's view, working-class women were the least educated, the least politically connected, and therefore the least useful women they could have in their organization. "Surely it is a mistake to use the weakest for the struggle!" Christabel allegedly told Sylvia. "We want picked women, the very strongest and most intelligent!"[15] Emmeline steadfastly supported the elder daughter, conspiring with Christabel to expel Sylvia from the WSPU and compelling the outcast daughter to turn the East London Federation of the Suffragettes into a separate organization.[16]

The schism between Sylvia and her mother and sister, apparent on the eve of the war, grew wider after 1914, when Emmeline and Christabel became flag-waving warmongers while Sylvia became an outspoken pacifist. The scene from Richard Attenborough's *Oh! What a Lovely War* (1969) in which Sylvia (played by Vanessa Redgrave) makes an anti-war speech to a hostile crowd of patriots depicts the younger Pankhurst daughter taking a stance directly opposed to that of her sister and mother.

The epilogue to the wartime dispute is even more revealing. Following the war, Emmeline became a member of the Conservative Party, a nationalist, and a staunch anti-communist; Christabel became a distinguished member of the Second Adventist movement, lecturing and writing books on the Second Coming; while Sylvia, at the opposite end of the political spectrum, became a prominent socialist, an anti-imperialist, and an anti-fascist.

In her unsympathetic film review on the World Socialist Web Site—a review provocatively subtitled "What Do Mrs Pankhurst and an East End Laundress Have in Common?" (the implication being that they have nothing in common)—Joanne Laurier takes Gavron to task for privileging the reactionary Emmeline Pankhurst over her socialist daughter.[17] However, although Sylvia does not appear as such in the film, the Alice Haughton character's role in the movie strongly evokes the part that the younger Pankhurst daughter played in the women's suffrage movement. Sylvia's East End campaign began in October 1912, more or less when the movie's Alice Haughton enters into Bethnal Green to recruit working women from the Glasshouse Laundry. This surrogate Sylvia Pankhurst character actually plays a bigger and more central role in the narrative than the Emmeline Pankhurst character does. Moreover, beyond this insertion of a pivotal Sylvia Pankhurst-like figure into the film, the socialist Pankhurst daughter's perspective permeates the film. The decision to recount the story from the point of view of lower-class women working in a commercial laundry aligns the film's politics with Sylvia's commitment to the working class, not Emmeline's complicity with the ruling class. The film's overall political position strongly favors Sylvia's sociopolitical stance over the one taken (already in the years 1912–13, but even more so in the years that followed) by her mother, despite the fact that the mother is the only Pankhurst character to appear as such on the screen.

As many social historians have pointed out, Sylvia Pankhurst's commitment to the working-class movement eventually overshadowed her dedication to the sole cause of women's rights. Although she originally entered into neighborhoods like Bethnal Green with the aim of recruiting women to the suffragette movement, she ended up "[leading] East End women in the direction of socialism."[18] The transformation of the East London Federation of Suffragettes into the Workers' Suffrage Federation, which in turn morphed into the Workers' Socialist Federation, is symptomatic of this shift in orientation. As Laurier writes in her film review, "From her own experiences with women like Maud Watts, Sylvia came to the conclusion that the problem was capitalism."[19]

Laurier concludes her thought-provoking film analysis by evoking a study by a UK think tank that in 2013 concluded that "'fifty years of feminism' has seen the gap between the wages of the average man and woman narrow, while the differences between working class and upper class women 'remain far greater than the differences between men and women.'"[20] Although there remains much progress to be made in the struggle for social equality between men and women, I agree with Laurier's overall conclusion that the defining battle of our time—the battle that the left has been progressively losing, rather than incrementally winning over the past 50 years or so—is the class war between the rich and the poor.

Class Struggle vs. Identity Politics

As a test case for this thesis, consider Simone de Beauvoir's famous pronouncement in the introduction to *The Second Sex* to the effect that, in contrast to the working class and African Americans, women do not conceive of themselves as a collective social group. Writing in the late 1940s, Beauvoir asserts:

Proletarians say "we." So do blacks [by which she means specifically African Americans]. Positing themselves as subjects, they thus transform the bourgeois or whites into "others." Women—except in certain abstract gatherings such as conferences—do not use "we"; men say "women," and women adopt this word to refer to themselves; but they do not posit themselves authentically as Subjects.[21]

Reading these sentences today, what leaps off the page is as much the confidence with which Beauvoir unequivocally states, as if it were self-evident, that proletarians say "we" as it is the more controversial proposition that women do not. The contrast that Beauvoir sets up between workers' solidarity and women's lack thereof (I will return to the case of African Americans in the following chapter) enables us to appreciate simultaneously the decline of working-class consciousness since the mid-twentieth century and the increase in gender identity since that time. It is proletarians who do not say "we" in the twenty-first century, not women. The situation has changed to such an extent since Beauvoir's time that we could retain her assessment virtually verbatim, with a few minor adjustments, by switching the words "proletarians" and "women."

Granted, the universal category of "women" to designate a discrete social group remains hotly contested within feminist circles. Since the publication of Kimberle Crenshaw's "Demarginalizing the Intersection of Race and Sex" in 1989, intersectionality—the theory that various biological and socio-cultural categories (race, class, gender, sexual orientation, ability, and so forth) constitute intersecting axes that form a person's social identity—has become a watchword in women's studies.[22] However, I would argue, intersectional theory could be advanced only at a time when the universal category of "women" had already achieved a certain ideological hegemony. The critique of this all-encompassing category—a category that lumps together women of different racial and ethnic backgrounds, with different sexual identities, belonging to different social classes, and so forth—bears witness to a previous ideological victory on the part of the radical feminists of the 1960s and 1970s, who presented themselves as a stand-in for the group as a whole and fought on behalf of this generic group.

One of the rare instances in which lefty-liberal academics and activists refer to social class on a regular basis in the twenty-first century is when they list it among identity attributes like those evoked above. What such lists of social attributes (race, class, gender, sexual preference, and the like) elide is a fundamental difference between the class struggle and identity-based activism. Slavoj Žižek characterizes this difference in the following terms: "In the first case [that of 'feminist, anti-racist, anti-sexist and other such struggles'], the goal is to translate antagonism into difference (the peaceful coexistence of sexes, religions, ethnic groups), while the goal of the class struggle is precisely the opposite, to turn class differences into class antagonisms."[23] I would push this argument further. In contrast to contemporary anti-racism, anti-sexism, anti-homophobia, anti-ableism, and so forth, which fight for recognition of and respect for historically marginalized social groups, the class struggle entails an irreducible antagonism between structurally opposed adversaries. In capitalism, one group's gain is the other's loss. The capitalist class strives to increase its profits at the expense of the working class, while workers fight to improve their standard of living at the capitalist's expense. This conflict between the competing interests of capital and labor is one of the foundational contradictions of capitalism, irrespective of what the individuals involved might feel toward one another. Although class compromises can be (and have been) reached, the underlying logic of the class structure is one of antagonism. The reason for this intrinsic antagonism is because, unlike struggles against racism, sexism, and the like, which combat *discrimination*, class warfare concerns *exploitation*. The two phenomena can and often do overlap, but they are fundamentally different. Respecting someone who is economically disadvantaged is perfectly compatible with championing the system that puts her at a disadvantage.

One of the merits of *Suffragette* in the current context is its recasting of feminism as a form of ideological warfare. By returning to a time when women in Britain were engaged in open combat with their oppressors, the film encourages us to rethink current forms of social engagement along the lines presented in the movie. In this regard, the filmmakers' strategic decision to center their story on working-class women from the East End serves a twofold function. I call this decision "strategic" because it is historically misleading. "It was in [...] middle-class discontent, rather than among working-class women, that the core of the feminist movement was formed" in Britain, social historian Paul Thompson writes in his authoritative 1975 study of Edwardian England.[24] What this strategic decision on the filmmakers' part permits is, on the one hand, a reconfiguration of feminism as a conflict between structurally opposed adversaries. The women's struggle operates, in the film, according to a logic of antagonism, as opposed to "a horizontal logic of the recognition of different identities."[25] In sum, it resembles the inherently antagonistic dynamic of class struggle more than the prevailing forms of multicultural feminism. On the other hand, the detailed illustration of hardships endured by a group of manual laborers working in a commercial laundry at the beginning of the last century enables the spectator to mentally link the working conditions depicted in *Suffragette* to the rampant exploitation of working women in the twenty-first century. In addition to taking us back to a time when feminists threw rocks through shop windows, blew up letterboxes, bombed empty buildings, and marched on Parliament in an effort to make their voices heard, the movie also brings the working women of the

Glasshouse Laundry into our world—a world where millions of young women toil in unspeakable conditions for pennies an hour in order to satisfy the needs of Western consumers. In the remainder of this chapter, I propose to examine the image that the film provides of labor, to relate that image to contemporary working conditions in the so-called Export Processing Zones around the world, and to explore the hypothetical solution that the film proffers to the problems it presents.

Images of Labor

That *Suffragette* intertwines the themes of exploitation and discrimination is apparent from the film's opening shots. The movie begins with the rhythmic sound of a steam engine chugging at a steady pace as the image slowly fades in from black to a close-up of a large whirring gear. The camera moves in a circular motion, tracing an arc slightly wider than the spinning gear, to reveal a steam-filled room and the blurry figure of a woman working in the background. It then cuts 180 degrees, showing the sweat-drenched back of the laboring woman as the whirring gear, which we now see is attached to a drive belt leading up to the ceiling, continues to spin. A series of shots embellish these introductory images. We see perspiring women in sweat-stained clothes loading bed sheets into industrial cylinders, scrubbing laundry on washboards, and ironing clothes on worktables. Through thick clouds of steam we perceive an intricate network of iron pipes and drive belts above the women's heads. Overlooking the scene, from an office situated off a catwalk above the shop floor, a man, later identified as Mr Taylor, tranquilly lights his pipe as he gazes down through a streaked window onto the factory floor below. As these images pass before our eyes, we hear numerous arguments (slightly rephrased versions of actual arguments advanced by Members of Parliament) against women's suffrage: "Women do not have the calmness of temperament or the balance of mind to exercise judgment in political affairs," one MP intones in voice-over. "If we allow women to vote, it will mean the loss of social structure," another opines. "Once the vote was given, it would be impossible to stop at this. Women would then demand the right of becoming MPs, cabinet ministers, judges," a third honorable member argues as the image of Taylor sucking on his pipe fades to black and the film title appears on the screen.

This rich and evocative scene, which sets up the narrative to come, economically conveys the two types of oppression that, combined, form the film's ideological battlefront. From it we infer, before the film narrative proper begins, that the movie amalgamates political inequality and an inequitable division of labor. Although we later learn that men also work at the laundry, the fact that these inaugural images present only women on the factory floor has the effect of fusing sexual discrimination and class exploitation in our imagination. Conversely, on the other side of the gender divide, the scene also implicitly relates the perspective of the male supervisor, who literally looks down on the women, to the positions advanced by the men that we hear in voice-over, who metaphorically "look down on" women. The gendered division of labor that we see on the screen and the inequitable distribution of political power that we hear the men upholding on the audio track combine to create the impression of a double oppression.

The magnificent set for the Glasshouse Laundry—an old print factory that production designer Alice Normington turned into a working vintage industrial laundry—transposes the social dynamic explored in the film onto the physical space of the factory.[26] The spatial organization of the laundry, inspired in spirit if not in architectural design by the Enlightenment-era social theorist Jeremy Bentham's concept of the Panopticon, enables Taylor to monitor the actions of his workers on the floor below at any time. As Michel Foucault writes in his famous study of "panopticism" in *Discipline and Punish* (1975), the

Panopticon (a building design in which a central tower enables a single watchman to observe all of a prison's inmates without them knowing whether or not they are being watched) "must be understood as a generalizable model for functioning." Citing Bentham, Foucault writes of the Panopticon: "It is—necessary modifications apart—applicable 'to all establishments whatsoever.'"[27] In addition to schools, mental institutions, and prisons, Foucault names, in particular, factories.[28]

Gavron and Morgan's decision to cast the working women in *Suffragette* as laundresses is an interesting one. Of the various professions that women practiced at the time, large-scale commercial laundry is among the ones that most closely resemble industrial labor. The striking opening shot of the whirring gear—an unexpected way to begin a film about the women's suffrage movement—renders this resemblance explicit. The follow-up shots of the women working the machinery and manipulating the tools of their trade beneath the intricate network of pipes, belts, and pulleys look like an illustration of the category that Karl Marx called the "productive forces" of labor, a category that includes both the means of labor (tools, machinery, infrastructure, and so forth) and human labor power.

However, although the scenes set in the Glasshouse Laundry *look like* depictions of productive labor, the women actually work in the service industry (they provide a service rather than manufacturing goods). This superimposition of one type of labor onto another reflects yet another strategic decision on the filmmaker's part. As the late journalist and political activist Chris Harman argues in *Zombie Capitalism*, "The usual distinction between 'industry' and 'service' obscures more than it reveals":

Some of the shift from "industry" to the "service sector" amounts to no more than a change in the name given to essentially similar jobs. Someone (usually a man) who worked a typesetting machine for a newspaper publisher

30 years ago would have been classified as a particular sort of industrial worker (a "print worker"); someone (usually a woman) working a word processing terminal for a newspaper publisher today will be classified as a "service worker."[29]

Suffragette takes a similar position by approaching the problem from the opposite direction. Rather than calling attention to the ways that jobs formerly classified as "industry" (jobs typically performed by men) have been redefined as "service jobs" (often performed by women), Gavron depicts women doing service work that strongly resembles industrial labor. Instead of calling into question the so-called "feminization of labor," as Harman does, Gavron presents an image of what Marxist feminist Nina Power evocatively calls, in her scathing critique of contemporary "feel-good" feminism, "the laborization of women."[30]

By conflating industrial labor and service work, Gavron effectively combines the two broadly defined domains of employment that women from the developing world have come to occupy in large numbers in recent decades. As sociologist Saskia Sassen demonstrates in her "Notes on the Incorporation of Third World Women into Wage Labor through Immigration and Offshore Production," globalization has encouraged two interrelated phenomena that together constitute "a new phase in the history of women."[31] On the one hand, with the deindustrialization of the formerly industrial West, multinational corporations, in pursuit of cheaper labor, laxer regulations, and lower taxes, have moved production to places more hospitable to business interests than the traditionally unionized, tightly regulated, and relatively progressively taxed regions of Western Europe and North America. These relocations have drawn a new pool of wage laborers—Third World women—into the workforce in unprecedented numbers. On the other hand (and as a result of the same global dynamic, which has disrupted traditional ways of life in the industrializing countries), immigrants from the Global

South have increasingly entered into the low-wage workforce in the Global North to perform service work that cannot be offshored and must be performed on location in the more affluent countries. This phenomenon likewise accounts for the employment of record numbers of Third World women, many of whom are entering into the wage-labor market for the first time.[32] In her depiction of women doing service work that looks like industrial labor, Gavron situates the working women of the Glasshouse Laundry at the interface of these two broadly defined categories of work, enabling the spectator to perceive the laundresses alternately or simultaneously as service workers or industrial laborers. In so doing, she subtly invites us to mentally link the conditions depicted in the film to those of innumerable women around the world in this "new phase in the history of women."

In *No Logo*, a penetrating study of capitalist globalization at the end of the twentieth century, Canadian author and social activist Naomi Klein offers a stark image of what those conditions look like for women working in the manufacturing sector of the global economy. Her account bears an uncanny resemblance to the work environment depicted in *Suffragette*. Here is Klein's description, based on interviews she conducted, of the untaxed, non-unionized, and self-regulated Export Processing Zones (EPZs) that currently employ (according to the International Labour Organization's conservative 2014 estimate[33]) over 66 million people:

> Regardless of where the EPZs are located, the workers' stories have a certain mesmerizing sameness: the workday is long—fourteen hours in Sri Lanka, twelve hours in Indonesia, sixteen in Southern China, twelve in the Philippines. The vast majority of the workers are women, always young [...]. The management is military-style, the supervisors often abusive, the wages below subsistence and the work low-skill and tedious.[34]

Gavron's depictions of the working women at the Glasshouse Laundry resemble Klein's account here so strongly that they could almost be a transposition of working conditions in a contemporary EPZ onto a fictional laundry in Edwardian England. Like in the EPZs, where "the vast majority of the workers are women, always young," most of the employees that we see at the laundry are young women. We recall in this context that Maud began working part-time at the laundry when she was 7 years old and full-time from the age of 12, becoming head washer by the age of 17 and forewoman at 20. She is 24–25 at the time of the film action, the standard cut-off age for women working in an EPZ.[35] Similarly, we learn that Violet started working at the laundry when she was 13, and her 12-year-old daughter, Maggie (Grace Stottor), already works there. The skeptical reader might object at this point that labor laws passed in industrialized countries have put an end to the sort of child labor we see in *Suffragette*, but, as Klein's study brings to light, the practice is widespread in the no-man's land of the EPZs. Klein cites innumerable examples of household, brand-name Western corporations (including Disney, Nike, Starbucks, and many others) that depend on child labor to produce their goods in the tax-free, self-regulated, and unmonitored labor havens that have been multiplying around the world since the 1980s.[36]

The abusive supervisors that Klein mentions in her account take a graphic form in the figure of Taylor, whose abusive behavior includes the sexual abuse of young girls in his employ. Maud was one of his previous conquests, the film strongly implies, and he now has his sights set on 12-year-old Maggie.

In her testimony at the House of Commons, Maud evokes the long hours that the women work and the menial compensation they receive for their labor: "We get thirteen shillings a week, sir. For a man it's nineteen and we work a third more the hours." The scenario that the laundress describes here conjures an image of the long workdays and the inadequate pay (as low as $0.16 an hour[37]) that Klein brings to light in her book. In sum, combining the images that we see of Maud and her coworkers, on the one hand, and the information that we gather from the dialog, on the other, we could imaginarily insert the laundresses of *Suffragette* into a contemporary EPZ and—obvious differences of dress and skin color aside—hardly notice the difference.

The hostile reception that Alice Haughton receives when she ventures into Bethnal Green in an effort to recruit working women to the suffragettes' cause also bears resemblance to the welcome that agitators receive in an EPZ. As Klein recounts, "there is a widely understood—if unwritten—'no union, no strike' policy inside the zones."[38] One particular site she visited— the Cavite Export Processing Zone, the largest free-trade zone in the Philippines—had a large sign in capital letters posted at its central intersection: "DO NOT LISTEN TO AGITATORS AND TROUBLE MAKERS."[39] In *Suffragette*, management does not even have to post such a sign. The workers at the laundry obey its dictate of their own accord. When scowls, heckling, and laughter do not deter Alice from delivering her message, an unsympathetic woman in the crowd translates the workers' overall sentiment into unambiguous terms for her: "Go home."

The tacit "no union, no strike" policy in force at the EPZs is by no means unique to free-trade zones. Management has always met attempts to unionize workers with stiff resistance. The tumultuous history of organized labor in Europe and North America in the late nineteenth and early twentieth centuries, when those regions were going through a phase of rapid industrialization, bears witness to the lengths to which capital has been willing to go in order to prevent workers from unionizing. Yet this history also shows the lengths to which labor organizers have gone in their efforts to mobilize workers. What characterizes the recent history of capital-labor relations is the decisive turn in capital's favor that those relations have taken. Since the neoliberal revolution of the 1980s, "no union, no strike" has become the prevailing *doxa* in industrial-labor relations, espoused even by segments of the working population that 50 years ago would have comprised card-carrying union members.[40]

In this context of disempowered labor and declining working-class consciousness, Gavron's depiction of an outside agitator who enters into the working-class neighborhood of Bethnal Green in order to mobilize a group of working women transcodes, for a class-blind era, the activities of a labor organizer.[41] The lengths to which the filmmaker goes to link women's political oppression with the laundress' socioeconomic situation make this allegorical dimension hard to miss. By the same token, the suffragettes' diverse modes of engagement in the film take on the appearance of a political general strike on the women's part. The mass rallies, the marches on Parliament, the violent clashes with police, the ostracism that Maud and Violet face at home and at work (culminating in their dismissal from the laundry and, in Maud's case, the loss of her family), the imprisonment and abuse that the women suffer, and their return to the ongoing struggle upon release from prison come across as episodes in a battle over both political rights and what nineteenth-century socialists called "the social question."[42]

In case the visual information on the screen does not sufficiently forge the link between the political and the socioeconomic domains in the viewer's imagination, Gavron has Maud cast the rabble-rousing Alice Haughton's speech outside the factory as a labor grievance when she recounts the scene to Sonny: "You see Mrs Haughton today?" she asks him. "Wants some of the women to go to Parliament. She thinks we should be paid more." In the scene we see of Alice addressing the crowd, the orator herself presents the problem as one of political rights: "We have an opportunity to demonstrate that as women are equal to men in their labors, so they should be equal to men in their right to vote." Thematically as well as visually, the film combines the political and the social realms, presenting them as two facets of a single configuration.

Demonstrating Equality

The logic of Alice's argument in the speech cited above—in effect, women are already equal to men, so they should therefore have equal rights—calls to mind French feminist Olympe de Gouges' famous syllogism in article 10 of her polemical *Déclaration des droits de la femme et de la citoyenne* (Declaration of the Rights of Woman and [Female] Citizen) of 1791. Remarking that the recently adopted *Déclaration des droits de l'homme et du citoyen* (Declaration of the Rights of Man and Citizen) extended universal suffrage to all Frenchmen, she impertinently asked whether French women were included in the category of "Frenchmen." The women were clearly French citizens, and yet they were denied a universal right guaranteed to the *hommes et citoyens* of the newly formed Republic. The rationale for the exclusion of women from the political arena, echoed by the Members of Parliament whose arguments we hear in voice-over in the opening scene of *Suffragette*, was that they belong to the private sphere of the home, rather than the public space of politics. However, de Gouges argued, the fact that women can be tried and sentenced to death as enemies of the state gives the lie to this relegation of women to the domestic sphere. If women are "entitled" to die on the scaffold, she famously argued, then they are already political subjects in the eyes of the law and should therefore enjoy the rights that the Declaration extends to members of that group: "Women have the right to mount the scaffold, they must also have the right to mount the speaker's rostrum."[43] Unfortunately, the government at the time could not hear (or, more to the point, refused to hear) the logic of this argument. De Gouges was executed by guillotine as a political dissident in 1793.

Jacques Rancière, who returns repeatedly to Olympe de

Gouges' syllogism in his writings, offers a sharp and incisive reading of this mode of argumentation. In his view, what the author of the Declaration of the Rights of Woman accomplishes is a twofold demonstration. On the one hand, her pamphlet illustrates that she does not have the rights that the official Declaration guarantees her as a French citizen. On the other hand, she shows, by her public action, that she in fact does have the rights that she has been denied on the grounds of her sex. In Rancière's terse formulation, feminists like de Gouges "acted as subjects that did not have the rights that they had and had the rights that they had not."[44] The formulation is paradoxical only in appearance. De Gouges exercised a right that she did not legally have and in so doing demonstrated that she in fact already possessed the right that the government refused to give her. In Rancière's interpretation, the content of de Gouge's argument and her mode of engagement are therefore inseparable. By presupposing that she was equal to men and acting like their equal, she demonstrated that she was in fact their political equal, thereby undermining the grounds for her exclusion from the public sphere.

The women in *Suffragette* engage in a comparable twofold demonstration. As Alice states in her speech outside the Glasshouse Laundry, working women are already equal to men in their labor. They should therefore have equal rights and equal pay. Moreover, the mere fact that she is in the street making speeches, handing out pamphlets, and rallying women demonstrates that she is a political being. Both the form and the content of her public oration refute the argument that women are private beings whose domain is restricted to the domestic sphere, an argument voiced by an MP at the beginning of the movie, who assures his esteemed colleagues that "women are well represented by their fathers, brothers, husbands." Numerous other characters in the film, from foot soldiers like Maud, Violet, and Edith to the demagogic Emmeline Pankhurst, enact similar twofold demonstrations. Even the politically motivated acts of sabotage and vandalism function as demonstrations of women's equality with men as fully politicized subjects.

In *Disagreement*, Rancière explicitly links this mode of argumentation to the workers' fight for the right to unionize and go on strike in nineteenth-century France:

> When French workers, at the time of the bourgeois monarchy [1830–48], ask the question, "Are French workers French citizens?" (in other words, "Do they have the attributes recognized by Royal Charter as those of Frenchmen equal before the law?"), or when their feminist "sisters" at the time of the Republic, ask the question, "Are Frenchwomen included in the 'Frenchmen' who hold universal suffrage?" both workers and women are starting with the gap between the egalitarian inscription of the law and the spaces where inequality rules.[45]

The French workers that Rancière alludes to here include groups like the Parisian tailors that went on strike in 1833 (a group studied in greater depth elsewhere in Rancière's work[46]). These workers were prohibited from unionizing and engaging in collective bargaining even though their bosses were allowed to form an association promoting their own interests. Yet the preamble to the Charter of 1830, the national governance document that the July Monarchy (or "bourgeois monarchy," as it came to be called) had recently promulgated, states that all French citizens are equal. By going on strike, the tailors forced the government to make a decision. Lawmakers could either respect the Charter, in which case they must allow the workers to exercise their rights, or else they could proscribe the tailors' union, in which case "the preamble of the Charter must be deleted. It should read: the French people are not equal."[47]

The potential for this mode of argumentation in the current

context is inestimable. In an era when an ever-increasing number of the world's governments tout the values of freedom and democracy while simultaneously disempowering the people and busting unions, calling attention to the discrepancy between what a government says it represents and what it actually does has the potential to disrupt the neoliberal consensus that rules the day. The Occupy Wall Street movement staged such a dissensus in exemplary fashion when, on September 17, 2011, a group of several thousand demonstrators began a months-long encampment protest in Manhattan's Zuccotti Park. The movement's powerful rallying slogan, "We are the 99 percent," eloquently drew attention to the contradiction between a globally hegemonic form of government that claims to be democratic and an international state of affairs in which the super-rich oligarchs (the 1 percent) control a grossly disproportionate share of the world's wealth and exercise inordinate political power. The message resonated around the world. By mid-October 2011, occupy protests had occurred or were currently underway in nearly a thousand cities around the world.

However, this mode of argumentation has its limits. As seen in chapter 1, the Occupy movement changed nothing. Wealth inequality has become more pronounced since the days of the Occupy movement; the corporatocracy of the 1 percent has become even more powerful. It is here that the second mode of political activism depicted in *Suffragette* becomes indispensable. The film's Edith Ellyn sums up this mode of engagement when she tells Maud, toward the beginning of the laundress's political education, that, as Mrs Pankhurst says, "It's deeds, not words, that will get us the vote." Or, as the movie's Violet Miller says in an early scene, in response to Maud's assertion that smashing windows is "not respectable": "Strangle what's respectable. You want me to respect the law, then make the law respectable." Maud eventually does strangle what is respectable. By leading us, along with Maud, who functions as our proxy in the film, from a position of skepticism to an embrace of militancy, Gavron invites us to follow her itinerary.

The violent and openly confrontational mode of engagement that the film proffers will not be to everyone's liking. The idea of throwing stones through windows and setting fire to politicians' residences is sure to be met with skepticism, even among people disillusioned with the neoliberal status quo. But in an era when democratically elected governments flagrantly disregard the manifest will of the people or propose, at best, band-aid solutions while simultaneously exacerbating the problem by pushing through new trade deals that benefit an international capitalist class at the expense of the rest of the world's population, the recourse to civil disobedience might be what is required. If, as Emmeline Pankhurst famously declared in 1912, "the argument of the broken pane is the most valuable argument in modern politics," it may be time to start breaking windows.[48] Maud and her cohort of militant suffragettes take this lesson to heart, and perhaps we should too.

Chapter 4

The Insurrection to Come: *Django Unchained*

In a three-part interview with historian and literary critic Henry Louis Gates Jr., filmmaker Quentin Tarantino responds to questions that his interviewer asks him about *Django Unchained* (2012), Tarantino's spaghetti Western about an African American slave turned retributive gunslinger in the antebellum US South. At one point, Gates asks his interviewee what motivated him to make a movie representing the suffering of slaves during the pre-Civil War era. Tarantino gives a roundabout answer that begins by explaining that prior to making the picture, he was writing film criticism on Italian filmmaker Sergio Corbucci (1926–90), whose *Django* (1966) is one of Tarantino's primary intertexts in *Django Unchained*. The interviewee says that no filmmaker's vision of the Wild West is as brutal and merciless as Corbucci's, and then proceeds to offer a three-step response to Gates' question, moving from an allegorical interpretation of Corbucci's ultraviolent cowboy movies to his decision to rework the Corbucci Western in a feature film of his own and finally to the choice to set his version of *Django* in the Deep South during the antebellum period. "I was working on a piece on Sergio Corbucci," Tarantino explains.

> And it really did seem like in his cowboy pictures what he truly was dealing with was fascism—which makes sense, as Italy was getting out from under Mussolini's boot heel not so long ago—just gussied up with cowboy-Mexican iconography. Even when his outlaws would take over a town or something, it had the feeling of a Nazi occupation, and with Holocaust-like suffering to the victims.
>
> So I'm writing all this, and part of the thing that's fun

about subjective criticism is it doesn't really matter what the director was thinking. It's about you making your point. So at some point I was like, I don't really know what Sergio Corbucci was thinking at the time, but I know I'm thinking it now, and I can do it.

And with that in mind, this violent, pitiless Corbucci West: What would be the American equivalent of that—that really would be real—that would be an American story? It was being a slave in the antebellum South.[1]

This explanation of the genesis of *Django Unchained* provides a fine point of entry into the film. It offers a nice glimpse into the way that Tarantino interprets films and how he incorporates them into his movies while providing a critical lens through which to view his own cinematic production.

In his response to Gates' question, Tarantino clearly communicates that, in his eyes, Corbucci's story of an ex-Union soldier who confronts a Ku Klux Klan-like gang operating on the Texas-Mexico border allegorizes resistance to fascism and Nazism. He is equally clear that he offers this interpretation based on his appreciation of the film, not on an understanding of the filmmaker's intentions. "It doesn't really matter what the director was thinking," Tarantino asserts. The statement also comes across as self-reflexive, inviting viewers to approach his movie in the same allegorical spirit that he adopted in viewing Corbucci's Westerns.

Tarantino then segues from a discussion of Corbucci's original *Django* to his own *Django* project: "I don't really know what Sergio Corbucci was thinking at the time, but I know I'm thinking it now, and I can do it." Following the tradition of film critics turned filmmakers like the *Cahiers du Cinéma* group of the 1950s who became the French New Wave directors of the early 1960s, Tarantino shifts here from a critical analysis of a genre film to the idea that he can "interpret" the genre in a film of his own.

Like the young Jean-Luc Godard, whose writings on Hollywood B movies and classic American film noir in the pages of the *Cahiers du Cinéma* anticipated his playful cinematic "essays" on the gangster genre in films like *À bout de souffle* (*Breathless*, 1960), *Bande à part* (*Band of Outsiders*, 1964), and *Alphaville* (1965), Tarantino presents *Django Unchained* as an audio-visual interpretation—a veritable critical essay on celluloid—of the spaghetti Western.

Tarantino then recounts that, in approaching the idea of remaking Corbucci in the twenty-first century, he came up with the idea that the historical equivalent, in the United States, to Corbucci's fascist Italy would be the antebellum South. This last step in Tarantino's line of reasoning is curious. As he makes clear, for him, Corbucci's *Django* was responding to a recent historical phenomenon: fascism, which reigned in Italy, in one form or another, from 1922 to 1945 (the last 2 years as a puppet government of Nazi Germany). In 1966, the year that the original *Django* was released, this historical context would have been very much alive in the cultural memory of Italians. To find an equivalent moment in US history, however, Tarantino returns not to recent events but more than 150 years into the past, long beyond the living memory of anyone in the film audience, to the Old South on the eve of the Civil War. The unstated and perhaps unintended suggestion here is that race-based chattel slavery paradoxically remains, in the twenty-first century, a phenomenon of the recent past. Implicit in the logic of Tarantino's set of associations is the idea that the enslavement of African Americans in the pre-Civil War South haunts the US collective psyche as if it were part of the nation's living memory, similar to the way that the then very fresh memory of fascism haunted Italy in the 1960s.

This chapter follows the various leads that Tarantino presents here in his response to Gates' question. I pay attention, in my analysis of Tarantino's "postmodern, slave-narrative Western" (as Gates calls it), to the movie's formal, aesthetic, and technical aspects as well as to narrative, thematic, and ideological considerations.[2] These two sets of categories are so thoroughly intermeshed in *Django Unchained* that it is difficult to discuss one without referring to the other. Form and content are of course always inseparable in a work of art, but in *Django Unchained* the generic form is so integral to the narrative content that it takes on a signifying capacity of its own and functions as ideological content in its own right. In sum, the movie offers a fine example of what Fredric Jameson calls "the ideology of form."[3] It self-consciously lends itself to—indeed, almost screams out for—the type of critical analysis that Jameson proposes, in *The Political Unconscious*, in which "'form' is apprehended as content."[4]

The analysis begins with an examination of the movie's opening title sequence, which sets up the film's central themes while illustrating with blinding clarity how Tarantino incorporates the generic form of the Corbucci Western into his narrative of a slave's self-emancipation. I then recap the story, insisting that the movie does indeed recount the tale of a slave's self-emancipation, rather than his emancipation by a benevolent white person. I pay particularly close attention, in my plot summary, to a series of pivotal scenes in the development of Django's (Jamie Foxx's) character as he transitions from enchained slave to free man, from a free black man in the antebellum South to a swaggering African American gunslinger in slave territory, from swaggering gunslinger back to human chattel, and finally from chattel slave to an unstoppable force of retribution. Contrary to what the movie title suggests, Django is not just "unchained" in the film; he is *unleashed*.

I then examine the currency of this pre-Civil War narrative in the early twenty-first century and the ways that it evokes contemporary capitalism. This examination begins with a consideration of the relationship between wage labor and slave labor. Although the two phenomena produce incomparably different life experiences for the worker or the slave, they resemble one another in their common drive to extract as much wealth as possible from human labor. Marx's frequent comparisons of capitalism to slavery are not just rhetorical flourishes. Moreover, as Marx insists, the particularly brutal form of slavery that developed in the United States over the course of the nineteenth century occurred as a direct result of the growth of capitalism. The enslavement and exploitation of African Americans in the pre-Civil War South represents not only one of the most horrific examples of slavery in world history, but also the asymptotic horizon of capital's immanent drive to maximize profits at labor's expense.

I then argue that, with the development of the global labor market, capitalism has been moving ever closer to that asymptotic horizon over the past few decades. Enabling capital to move production to wherever labor is cheapest, taxes are lowest, and regulations weakest, globalization has permitted an international capitalist class to increase vastly its share of the world's wealth at the expense of everybody else. The phenomenon has led critical race theorist Cornel West and NPR talk show host Tavis Smiley to argue, in their aptly titled *The Rich and the Rest of Us*, that "poverty is the new slavery."[5] Given the increasingly large number of people who find themselves on the financial margins of capitalist societies—a population disproportionally represented, in the United States, by people of color, for reasons that I trace to specific policy decisions made by the Nixon and Reagan administrations during the post-civil rights years—I then consider the positions advanced by social and political thinkers from Marx and Engels in the nineteenth century to Pulitzer Prize-winning author and social activist Chris Hedges in 2015 to the effect that those on the lowest rungs of the social ladder do not lead revolutions but, rather, that revolutions come from disgruntled members of the privileged and semi-privileged classes. To this argument, David Harvey responds that, in the twenty-first century, the stirrings will more likely come from the growing ranks of "the wretched of the earth" than the discontented middle and upper-middle classes. It is the latter scenario, I argue, that *Django Unchained* allegorizes.

Political Pastiche

The movie begins with a static shot of a rocky desert landscape. We hear the opening bars of Luis Bacalov's "Django," the theme song for Corbucci's original film, as a series of titles informs us, in the same black-bordered red letterpress style font that Corbucci used for the opening title sequence of *Django*, that the Weinstein Company and Columbia Pictures present a film by Quentin Tarantino. The vocals kick in just as the first of the movie's five principal actors' names appears on the screen. When the last of the five stars' names appears, the camera begins a slow diagonal pan and tilt down and to the right to reveal a group of half a dozen shirtless black men with whip marks on their back, who trudge through the desert in a medium close-up. A gap in the formation enables us to perceive clearly the whipped back of Django, whose broad shoulders fill the right half of the frame. In unison with the pronunciation of the title character's name in the theme song, the word "Django" appears on the screen in Corbucci's stylistic "Western" letterpress font. The sound of a whip crack (not in Bacalov's original theme song), used here as percussion, accompanies the appearance on the screen of the word "unchained," written in plain white letters, giving us the full title of the film we are watching.

The remainder of the title sequence, which lasts the duration of Bacalov's ballad, shows two white men on horseback leading the six shackled slaves, who are silently reduced in number to five by the end of the sequence, first across the desert and then through a sparse forest. In following the group's progression, the sequence provides a mini-catalog of stunning film techniques that present themselves as such. It contains, for example, two snap zooms, one of Tarantino's signature cinematic devices, borrowed from the 1960s- and 1970s-era films that he quotes so freely in his movies. One of these sudden changes of scale is particularly striking. The shot begins as a smooth pan across a rocky desert vista at sunset. Superimposed on the image appear the words "and with the friendly participation of Franco Nero" (a reference to the actor who played the original Django in 1966). Just as the music on the sound track shifts from the chorus to a guitar interlude and the acknowledgment of Nero's participation vanishes from the screen, the camera freezes and does a super-fast zoom in on the procession of shackled men and the two slave traders on horseback as they pass, far in the background, between two massive rock formations in the middle ground. Throughout the sequence, each change of scale, each dramatic shift in focus, each transition from one type of shot to another, from one reframing technique to another, from daylight to nighttime, and from one setting to the next occurs in conjunction with musical cues on the sound track, and each is timed in unison with the appearance or disappearance of titles on the screen. The sequence as a whole is a self-consciously bravura performance of stylistic filmmaking that calls attention to its technical virtuosity while simultaneously communicating the diegetic situation in the film.

Numerous critics have called attention to the way that *Django Unchained*'s opening title sequence situates the film at the interface of two heterogeneous genres. Michael Johnson, for example, in his contribution to a special issue of *Safundi* dedicated to the movie, proposes that "the opening scene of *Django Unchained* provides in quick visual form a microcosm of the film's genre innovation— its 'poaching and borrowing' from two seemingly incompatible sources, the genre western and the story of slavery."[6] Making a similar point, Johannes Fehrle argues, in his contribution to the same issue of *Safundi*, that "the first few minutes of *Django Unchained* not only locate the film 'in movieland,' they also place it in history." The "movieland" to which Frehle refers here—a nod to film critic Richard Alleva's quip that *Django Unchained* "takes place in movieland, the only country Tarantino knows"— is primarily that of the spaghetti Western, whereas the "history," by contrast, is that of "slavery and race relations in the pre-Civil War US."[7] However, Frehle points out, it is not only the generic form of the 1960s Italian Western and the historical setting of the antebellum South that the sequence conjures, but the cinematic genre of the 1970s Blaxploitation film as well. Citing such films as Martin Goldman's *The Legend of Nigger Charley* (1972), Larry Spangler's *The Soul of Nigger Charley* (1973), and Jack Arnold's *Boss Nigger* (1975)—all three films starring Fred Williamson—as well as Richard Fleischer's *Mandingo* (1975), Frehle argues that Tarantino's film pays homage to (or, in the critic's estimation, rips off) the 1970s Blaxploitation genre. What the opening sequence presents, in these critics' opinion, is an introduction to Tarantino's generic pastiche, a pastiche that the filmmaker himself calls, in reference to the transposition of the "Western" genre onto a slave narrative set largely on cotton plantations in antebellum Mississippi and Tennessee, a "Southern."[8]

What these two heterogeneous film traditions have in common is a counterhegemonic stance in relation to a dominant power structure. Fehrle emphasizes the contestatory dimensions of the 1970s Blaxploitation film: "Thematically the genre is heir to the 1960s Civil Rights movement and the increasing radicalization of parts of the African American population in the late 1960s and early 1970s Black Power Movement."[9] Echoing Frehle here, Adilifu Nama writes, in his book on representations of race in Tarantino's films:

> In contrast to the established tradition of Hollywood films advancing trite and racist presentations of black enslavement [Nama names in particular D.W. Griffith's 1915 *Birth of a Nation*, David O. Selznick's 1939 production of *Gone with*

the Wind, and Disney's 1946 *Song of the South*], a wave of militant black slave films did crop up during the high tide of Blaxploitation films in the 1970s, having appropriated the last vestiges of political verve from a waning Black Power movement.[10]

Concerning the spaghetti Western, the other major genre that Tarantino cannibalizes in his film, Neil Campbell writes in a fascinating article on the enthusiastic reception of the original *Django* in post-colonial Jamaica: "Italian Westerns were already post-Westerns, knowing and critical, edgy, Marxist, and surreal."[11] Campbell cites in this regard a famous statement by Sergio Leone, the most celebrated of the Italian directors of 1960s cowboy movies: "As Romans, we have a strong sense of the fragility of empires. [...] That is what I have tried to show in my films. [...] I see the history of the West as really the reign of violence by violence."[12] Like the 1970s Blaxploitation movies, which implicitly contested white supremacy, the 1960s spaghetti Westerns, in Leone's view, called into question a dominant power's claim to power.

In incorporating the cinematic tropes of the spaghetti Western and the Blaxploitation film, Tarantino's film style conjures the oppositional political stances that these two different film genres present. Before or beyond the narrative development of *Django Unchained*, the movie encodes a counterhegemonic message by virtue of its hybrid generic form. The film form itself, in other words, bears ideological content and transmits ideological meaning. As Jameson writes in a very different context (that of a disquisition on literary history and criticism), "a dialectical reversal has taken place in which it has become possible to grasp [...] formal processes as sedimented content in their own right, as carrying ideological messages of their own, distinct from the ostensible or manifest content of the works."[13] Although Jameson himself would no doubt see little of critical value in Tarantino's work, as his dismissive comments on pastiche in particular and postmodern art in general make clear, his statement here is directly pertinent to thinking about a film like *Django Unchained*.[14] In the latter film, it is eminently possible to grasp formal processes "as sedimented content in their own right, as carrying ideological messages of their own."

In order to bring into relief the oppositional stance that Tarantino's aesthetic represents, we might engage in a bit of periodization. By situating his film in the lineage of the spaghetti Western and the Blaxploitation film, Tarantino in effect presents *Django Unchained* as a movie from the late 1960s or early 1970s made in 2012. As Jameson insists, the period generally known as "the sixties"—a period which, according to Jameson, "may be said to have begun (slowly) in 1963 [...] and to have ended dramatically somewhere around 1973–75"—was passionately political.[15] Jameson's periodization of "the sixties" here runs, not coincidentally, from the year before Leone's *A Fistful of Dollars* established the spaghetti Western as a major film genre in 1964 to the moment that the wave of Blaxploitation films crested in the mid-1970s. This period saw the emergence of not only the Vietnam-War protest movement, which "defined and constituted" the politics of the sixties, according to Jameson.[16] It was also the culmination of the civil rights movement in the United States, the heyday of the women's movement, and the apex of radical student engagement. It is the period that saw what, in retrospect, we now know to be the last heroic triumphs of the labor movement, nowhere more apparent than in the streets of Paris in May 1968, when some 11 million workers (more than 22 percent of the total population of France at the time) went on strike, joining ranks with student protestors and nearly bringing the de Gaulle government to its knees.

Tarantino's generic pastiche, his signature late 1960s–early 1970s film style, and even his steadfast refusal to make movies in digital format in an era when the vast majority of his peers have embraced the technology, transport the viewer to this time period when the fragility of empires was taken for granted and political positions were more than lifestyle choices or matters of personal identity. In sum, Tarantino's "movieland" is a place in which emancipatory politics and progressive social revolution were still considered possible. The ideological message formally transmitted in *Django Unchained*—the ideological content of the movie's generic form—is one of contestation. The technical and aesthetic dimensions of the film function as audio-visual signifiers (or what Danish linguist Louis Hjelmslev would call "connotators"[17]) in their own right, conjuring a spirit of revolt and fostering a desire for emancipation independent of the movie's narrative content.

Django Unleashed

I do not mean to downplay the film's narrative content, which has very much to do with emancipation and revolt. The addition of the adjective "unchained" to the title of *Django* signals immediately that the film is an emancipation narrative. However, the movie title is also misleading. Django is freed from bondage less than 10 minutes into the film, when Dr King Schultz (Christoph Waltz), a former German dentist now working as a bounty hunter in the American Southwest, buys him from one of the two slave traders that drove Django and his fellow prisoners through the desert in the film's opening title sequence (the other trader having been shot in the head by Schultz moments before). A close-up of Schultz's hands removing the leg irons from around Django's ankles offers a fine literal illustration of the film's title. If the movie set out to depict a slave's emancipation, it could end there. Django is "unchained" in the movie's second scene.

A colleague of mine self-effacingly said a few years ago, in reference to a French translation of a book that he had originally written in Arabic, that the French translation was better than his Arabic original. In a similar vein, I would argue that the

French translation of the title of *Django Unchained* is better than Tarantino's original title. *Django déchaîné* means two things. The adjective *déchaîné*, derived from the French word for "chain" and the privative prefix *dé-*, means literally "unchained," but it is used idiomatically to refer to relentless forces. In the latter sense, its usage is virtually identical to the idiomatic use of "unleashed" in English. What Tarantino gains in opting for "unchained" over "unleashed" is an association with the heavy weight and the clanking sound of chains; what he sacrifices is the connotation of an irrepressible force. The French title felicitously communicates both. While the former association produces a powerful sensory image, it is the latter connotation that is of utmost importance to understanding the film's politics, as I propose to show now by going through the plot in stages, examining key scenes and exploring ways that the mise-en-scène (especially Sharen Davis' magnificent costume designs) and the cinematography in the various scenes work in conjunction with the dialog to construct a narrative of self-emancipation and revolt, leading up to the demolition of the movie's primary symbol of oppression in its final scene.

The arc of the main character's development progresses in five distinct stages, each associated with a particular costume that Django wears and, in many cases, presented in a spectacular shot or series of shots that depicts the hero's transformation. The first such shot occurs immediately after Schultz unshackles Django. In the earliest of the film's many slow-motion shots, the unbound hero walks away from the group of chained slaves and toward the slave trader that Schultz has just shot, who now lies dead on the ground. As Django approaches the dead man, the camera follows him from behind in a medium shot that advances at the same pace as the freed slave. His body just off center in the frame, Django throws off his moth-eaten blanket, lifting and spreading out his arms like a bird of prey as he advances toward the slain trader. A cartoon-like whooshing noise accompanies

Django's gesture of throwing off his ratty blanket. The look of the slow-motion shot, reinforced by the exaggerated sound effect, imbues the image with an ominous power that goes beyond the narrative content of a man removing his covering as he walks. The shot creates the impression of Django shedding his slave identity as if it were a foul second skin while simultaneously anticipating the transformation of the freed slave into a figure of retribution.

Sporting the dead trader's cowboy hat, fur-lined wool coat, leather gloves, and cowboy boots (but still wearing the tattered canvas pants that he wore as a slave), Django rides off on the dead man's nag with Schultz, who drives a dental wagon adorned with a huge tooth sculpture that bounces back and forth on a ridiculous coil spring as the cart advances. The two men arrive in the town of Daughtrey, Texas, where they are ogled by townspeople who "ain't never seen no nigger on a horse before," as Django explains to Schultz. The expression that Django uses here captures his paradoxical position. Slaves in antebellum Texas had the legal status of personal property. They did not ride horses, a privilege reserved for legally defined "people." In riding a horse, Django is acting like a human being rather than chattel, and yet his legal status is that of the latter. This paradoxical status of a juridically nonhuman biped that nonetheless acts like a man returns as a leitmotif in the film. In the scene of the arrival in Daughtrey, the townspeople's reactions clearly communicate the extent to which they perceive the sight of an African American on horseback to be an anomaly. For them, "nigger on a horse" (an utterance pronounced in a tone of disbelief by one of the good people of Daughtrey upon seeing the spectacle of a black man on horseback) is a contradiction in terms. It makes no more sense, within their ingrained racist worldview, than an expression like "walking fish" or "dry rainy day."

A slow-motion high-angle tracking shot follows the duo's

progression down Daughtrey's main street from a perspective situated behind two men who look down from a balcony onto the pair below. As the camera follows the two riders, it moves past the onlookers into a position behind a noose that hangs from a porch rafter. The sinister atmosphere evoked in the shot is rendered explicit when Django passes in front of the noose. The camera perfectly frames the freed slave's head in the looped rope as he rides past it. The shot typifies Tarantino's aesthetic in this "Southern." Its iconography pays explicit homage to the classic spaghetti Westerns, which often begin with a cowboy riding past a noose or a row of coffins as he arrives in a hostile town. The scene sets us up for a piece of genre entertainment with the added twist of casting the main character as a black gunslinger in slave territory.

The movie's overall conformity to the genre of the Italian Western makes the next transformation in Django's appearance all the more jarring. Following Schultz's assassination of Daughtrey's sheriff—a former outlaw wanted for cattle rustling—the duo set out to find the Brittle brothers, three men who worked as overseers on the plantation that used to own Django. Like the Daughtrey sheriff, the Brittle brothers are wanted men with a price on their head. Schultz plans to track them down and collect the bounty on their head, but he does not know what they look like. The reason he recruited Django's help in the first place is because he presumed that the former slave knows them. In fact, we learn in a series of "spaghetti Western" flashbacks (staples of the genre, which depict the invariably traumatic prehistory of the protagonist), Django knows them all too well. It is they who whipped Django and his wife, Broomhilda (Kerry Washington), when the two of them were caught trying to escape from the plantation. A set of gruesome flashbacks, depicted in overexposed shots that give the scenes a washed-out look, shows the brothers tying Broomhilda to a tree and lashing her with a bullwhip as Django fruitlessly begs them to stop.

These various narrative details, presented in classic macaroni Western style, situate us in the world of the Tarantino "spaghetti Southern." They make the colorful outfit that Django sports in the first scene depicting him as an independent agent and a force of retribution in his own right seem all the more outrageous.

When Schultz prepares Django for the pursuit of the Brittle brothers, he explains to his apprentice that the two of them will be putting on an act as they go from plantation to plantation in Gatlinburg, Tennessee, looking for the three wanted men. During the act, Schultz explains, Django will be playing the role of the valet. The bounty hunter then asks his rookie sidekick to pick out a costume for his valet character. The first few measures of "His Name Was King" (the Luis Bacalov theme song for the 1971 spaghetti Western of the same title) culminate in a horn blast that marks a transition from the scene of Django and Schultz clothes shopping to the beginning of their quest for the Brittle brothers.

The Brittle brothers sequence begins with a series of shots of Django on horseback wearing a preposterous royal blue suit. The outfit, modeled on the costume worn by the subject in portraitist Thomas Gainsborough's *The Blue Boy* (ca. 1770), is composed of bright blue satin knee breeches and a matching jacket, complemented by a white lace neckerchief tied in a big bow around Django's neck.[18] The color of the flamboyant costume stands in sharp contrast to the somber shades that have characterized the film's color palette up to this point. Django looks like a character imported from a film of a completely different genre.

In her contribution to Oliver Speck's edited volume on *Django Unchained*, Margaret Ozierski proposes that the scenes of Django in his valet livery evoke the tradition of the eighteenth-century French playwright Pierre de Marivaux's comedies. In these theatrical pieces, Ozierski explains, "the figure of the valet is a savvy character who often shows more spirit and wit than his master."[19] The introductory shots of Django in his valet finery reinforce the idea that he has become the dominant member of the pair. Previous shots of the two men riding together generally showed Django riding either next to or behind Schultz. In sequential shots that showed first one of the men, then the other riding alone in the frame, a shot of the doctor driving his dental wagon always preceded a follow-up shot of Django on horseback. Breaking these patterns, the scene of the duo riding up to Big Daddy's (Don Johnson's) plantation in Gatlinburg begins with a series of shots showing Django leading Schultz down a path through a cotton field. As the pair progress, the slaves working the fields stop picking cotton, straighten their backs, and stare at the singular spectacle of an ostentatiously dressed Afro-American on horseback leading a white rider.

The idea that Django has become the dominant one of the pair, silently suggested by the camera's fixation on the valet in his fancy blue suit and buttressed by the images of the field hands who stop what they are doing to stare at him as he passes by, is borne out in the sequence that follows. Schultz had explained earlier to Django the general strategy for collecting the bounty on the Brittle brothers: "When we find them, you point them out and I kill them." This is not the way the scene plays out. Rather than Django pointing them out and Schultz killing them, Django has one of Big Daddy's house slaves point them out to him, and then he kills them (or, in any case, two of them, at which point Schultz arrives and shoots the third brother as he flees on horseback).

Ozierski and Nama offer insightful readings of the scene in which Django marches across the grounds of Big Daddy's plantation and interrupts Big John (MC Gainey) and Roger ("Little Raj") Brittle (Cooper Huckaby), who are preparing to whip Little Jody (Sharon Pierre-Louis), a house slave they are punishing for breaking eggs. Ozierski calls attention to the presence, in the traveling shot that follows Django as he marches across the grounds, of the figure of a young slave girl who sways on a swing suspended from a massive tree in the background. The presence, in this slave narrative, of Django in his *Blue Boy* outfit and the idyllic image of the swinging slave girl, whom Ozierski compares to the main figure in French Rococo painter Jean-Louis Fragonard's *The Swing* (1767), produces a surrealistic image that juxtaposes incompatible worlds: that of the *ancien régime* leisure class, on the one hand, and that of a brutal slave narrative set in the pre-Civil War South, on the other hand. "Through astute staging and mise-en-scène," Ozierski writes, "Tarantino brilliantly captures the sheer displacement of these annunciatory figures, who at once belong to the scene and are utterly foreign to it."[20]

Nama, for his part, interprets the scene of Blue Boy arriving to rescue Little Jody as an episode from a Gothic horror film (the genre to which *Django Unchained* belongs, in his opinion). Nama remarks that the shot showing Little Jody tied to the tree with her bare back exposed to Big John's whip offers us a glimpse of Django's reflection in a mirror leaning against a stack of bricks in the background. The striking feature of this shot, Nama points out, is that Django's hands and face are indiscernible in the reflected image. We see his blue suit and white neckerchief reflected in the glass, but the mirror does not reflect his flesh. "The effect, in that moment," Nama comments, "works to destabilize Django as a human representation and places him in the realm of living myth, a specter of righteous retribution."[21]

What I would add to these keen analyses, which call attention to the genre-bending aspects of the imagery, is, first of all, the way that the scene improbably returns to the spaghetti Western aesthetic in the shot that connects the two moments that Ozierski and Nama discuss. When Django finishes his march across the plantation grounds, he calls out John Brittle's name just as the overseer is about to strike his first blow against Little Jody. We then see, from a perspective situated more or less at Jody's eye level, a wide low-angle shot that pushes in to a medium long shot of Django as we hear a trumpet play the opening notes of Bacalov's "La Corsa." The Bacalov trumpet piece is from Corbucci's original *Django*, but in contrast to the ballad-type Bacalov songs that Tarantino borrows for *Unchained*, this instrumental piece is pure spaghetti Western, in the vein of Ennio Morricone's famous sound tracks for Leone's *Dollars Trilogy* (1964–66). Django's stance is also lifted directly out of the spaghetti Western playbook. He stands with his feet planted on the ground roughly two and a half feet apart, slightly wider than the width of his shoulders, and he holds his arms out slightly from his body, as if he were preparing to draw a six-gun from his non-existent holster. Moreover, the wide shot that slowly pushes in to the narrower view of Django in this stance culminates in what is sometimes referred to as a "cowboy shot," framing the figure from just above the head to just above the knee, so called because it enables the spectator to see both the actor's face and his holstered six-shooter in the frame. In sum, we are squarely in Tarantino's movieland, the world of the macaroni Southern, but the figure of righteous retribution is wearing an absurd bright blue costume modeled after the one worn by a prepubescent English boy in an oil painting that antedates the film's diegetic time period by nearly a century. What are we to make of this bizarre choice of costume?

Django's emancipation takes two distinct forms, both represented in the cowboy shot of Blue Boy in his showdown stance. The first is that of a vengeful figure of reprisal, or what Nama calls "a blatant example of the return of the repressed."[22] To convey this first form of emancipation, it is thematically and ideologically important that it is Django, not Schultz, who executes the two Brittle brothers that are preparing to beat Little Jody. As historian David Roediger writes in *Seizing Freedom*, his gripping account of the social impact of the nineteenth-century slave revolts in the United States: "The slave who freed himself or herself and then fought to free others was a particular symbol of possibility, the very embodiment of Lord Byron's 1812 injunction that those 'who would be free, themselves must strike the blow.'"[23] This idea, borrowed from Byron, that those who would be free must strike the blow themselves, takes crystalline visual form in the shots of Django bullwhipping Little Raj after having shot Big John with a derringer hidden up his sleeve. These bullwhipping shots, set to Bacalov's dramatic trumpet music, give cinematic form to an image like Henry Louis Stephens' *Blow for Blow*, a Civil War-era lithograph, reproduced in Roediger's book, depicting a black slave beating a white slaver with a stick.[24]

The second form that Django's emancipation takes is more "performative," in the sense that feminist and queer theorist Judith Butler lends to the term in her writings on gender performativity.[25] Django "performs" his freedom, acting, in essence, like a free man. This "performative" dimension of Django's emancipation is the one that the townspeople of Daughtrey found so scandalous when Django rode into town on horseback wearing a cowboy hat and a wool coat. However, the incongruity of the image of a black man on horseback, although blindingly obvious to the people of Daughtrey, is not so visually apparent to the twenty-first-century spectator. By contrast, the figure of an African American cowboy wearing bright blue knee breeches, a matching jacket, and a fancy lace collar is. The flashy costume functions, not only within the film narrative, but also in the viewer's imagination, as an index of Django's singularity and a sign of his emancipation.

The next stage in Django's character development brings together these two aspects of his emancipation. Having agreed to partner up for the winter and then set out together in the spring to look for Broomhilda, who was sold at a slave auction in Greenville, Mississippi, the freed slave and the retired dentist form a bounty hunting team. This "buddy movie" segment of the film begins (once again, in conjunction with the opening bars of a song, in this case, Jim Croce's folksy "I Got a Name") with a medium close-up of Schultz's muddy boots occupying the left side of the film frame and the lower portion of a porch door on the right. The door then swings open and we see Django's feet step out onto the porch in a pair of brand new black leather boots. The camera then does a pedestal shot moving up Django's legs and torso to a bust view of him in a striking cowboy outfit. Although Schultz shares the frame with the decked-out cowboy, the shot directs our attention to Django. We cannot even see the doctor's face, the brim of his hat covering his features as he admires his partner's new clothes, which consist of beige velvet pants, a green corduroy jacket, a stylish dark brown cowboy hat with a studded leather band, and a new cordovan holster with a shiny brass buckle. While the outfit is modeled on the one that Little Joe Cartwright (Michael Landon) wore in the 1960s and early 1970s TV series *Bonanza*, the shot is designed to reveal not only the costume in all its splendor, but the hero in all his glory. The vertical camera movement from toe to head aggrandizes the figure while inviting us to admire, along with Schultz, Django's stunning Little Joe Cartwright ensemble.

It is in this "dude" outfit, which Django sports for the next hour of the film, that the hero begins his next escapade with Schultz. Once again, Schultz explains to his partner that the two of them will be playing an act. The two men plan to pretend that they are shopping for a mandingo fighter—an apparently apocryphal reference to slaves that engaged in gladiator-like combat in the Old South—in order to gain entry into Candyland, the plantation that currently owns Broomhilda. Candyland's proprietor, Calvin Candie (Leonardo DiCaprio), is a mandingo enthusiast. The plan is to pretend to buy a mandingo fighter from Candie for the "ridiculous" price of $12,000 and then actually to buy Broomhilda as a side purchase while the details of the mock purchase are being worked out. In this charade, Schultz plays the role of the buyer while Django masquerades as a slaver with expertise in the mandingo fight game.

Django plays his part of a black slaver with authenticity and conviction. He goes so far as to bully Candie's slaves in order to demonstrate his superiority over them, to challenge openly Monsieur Candie in public, to pull a Candyland slave driver from his horse and throw him to the ground when the man dares to insult Django, and to equate brazenly Candie's lawyer—the obsequious Leonide Moguy (Dennis Christopher)—with the slaves in Candie's entourage. The act works like a charm, and everything proceeds according to plan until Stephen (Samuel L. Jackson), the head house slave at Candyland, intuits the relationship between Broomhilda and Django, and calls Calvin aside to explain what is going on. Candie then forces Schultz, at gunpoint, to buy Broomhilda for the "ridiculous" price of $12,000. In a final demonstration of his dominance over the outfoxed Schultz, Candie demands that the doctor shake his hand as a gesture of good faith. Schultz responds by shooting the odious plantation owner in the heart. Candie's bodyguard then kills Schultz with a shotgun blast, and an over-the-top gunfight breaks out in which Django kills a dozen and a half Candyland henchmen before Stephen intervenes, warning Django that they will kill Broomhilda if he does not surrender.

Significantly, Django's surrender is depicted in a shot of him ripping open his green corduroy jacket, popping the wooden buttons off the coat as he strips it from his body. A slow-motion close-up of the buttons bouncing off of the floorboards dramatizes the gesture, which serves no obvious diegetic function in the narrative. A follow-up shot from the same angle shows the jacket landing on the floor beside the buttons. These spectacular "vestimentary" shots take on their full significance in the following scene, in which Django hangs upside down from a rafter, naked except for an iron mask on his face and a G-string covering his crotch. The hero has been reduced here to the abject condition that Italian philosopher Giorgio Agamben calls "bare life": the pure, naked, unqualified existence of a biological entity with no legal status as a human being.[26] Tarantino graphically represents Django's reduction to *la vita nuda* by actually stripping him naked.

A turn of events enables Django to escape the bloody fate that his captors envision for him. In a plot development that risks coming across as a bad joke to members of the film audience that work for a living, Stephen, who has every intention of inflicting the most horrible punishment imaginable on Django, convinces Calvin's sister Lara (Laura Cayouette) that working all day, every day for a multinational mining company is a fate worse than being castrated to death, devoured by dogs, or any of the other gruesome tortures that the Candyland sadists fantasize for Django. Miss Lara therefore agrees to give Django to the LeQuint Dickey Mining Company, where, as Stephen maliciously explains to the captive slave, "henceforth, till the day you die, all day, every day, you will be swingin' a sledgehammer, turning big rocks into little rocks." However, en route to the mine, Django talks the three dimwitted LeQuint Dickey employees that are transporting him and three other Candyland slaves across the Mississippi countryside to cut him loose and give him a pistol so that he can help them kill and collect the bounty on a gang of outlaws that, he claims, are hiding out at Candyland. Django shoots the three numbskulls as soon as they give him a gun. He then heads off to Candyland for the final showdown, wiping out a posse of slave trackers and burning their outpost to the ground along the way.

The final showdown sequence begins with an offscreen tenor voice singing an a cappella version of "In the Sweet By and By" as we see Miss Lara, three gun-toting cowboys, and three loyal house slaves (Stephen among them) returning at night from Calvin's funeral. The mourners arrive at the "big house" of Candyland and enter into the foyer while the melodic hymn continues to play in the background. The flicker of a match from the upstairs balcony and a change in the singer's voice signal to us that the song that we had thought up until that point to be non-diegetic is in fact part of the diegesis. The match flicker and the change in the singer's tone also signal to the group below that the source of the song is none other than Django, who approaches the banister, looks down at the mourners, and informs them: "Y'all gonna be together with Calvin in the by and by, just a bit sooner than y'all was expecting." The last of the movie's gun battles takes place in a matter of seconds, during which Django dispatches the three cowboys with a few gun blasts. He then asks Cora (Dana Gourrier), the house mammy, to bid Miss Lara goodbye, and in the most cartoonish shot of the movie, blows the mistress of Candyland off the film set with a single gunshot. He then advises Cora and Sheba (Nichole Galicia), Candie's slave concubine, to run along, and he turns his attention to Stephen.

The first thing that Django does when he is alone with his archenemy is comment on his clothes. "Stephen!" he calls out. "How you like my new duds? You know, before now, I didn't know that burgundy was my color." The outfit is indeed quite fetching, consisting of a burgundy jacket with velvet lapels, a crisp white shirt with a winged collar, a silk tie, and a stylish gold lamé paisley waistcoat. The spectator may find herself at a loss to come up with an explanation for how Django came into possession of this elegant outfit. Did he stop at an upscale clothier on his way to Candyland in order to buy the perfect ensemble for the final showdown? If so (as far-fetched as that scenario already is), with what money did he buy the outfit? The more details one factors into this unlikely scenario, the more implausible it becomes. The sympathetic viewer might agree to suspend her disbelief and accept the idea that in movieland, people can miraculously appear in whatever clothing best suits a given scene. However, a logical explanation for this costume exists. No suspension of disbelief is required. Django's elegant burgundy ensemble is the same outfit that Calvin Candie wears in his first appearance on the screen: same burgundy jacket with the velvet lapels, same white shirt with the winged collar, same burgundy tie, same gold-on-burgundy lamé vest...Django even clenches Calvin's carved ivory cigarette holder between his teeth. Django presents himself for his final act of retribution in the guise of his ideological nemesis. The only parts of the costume that do not come from Candie's wardrobe are Django's gun belt and his signature cowboy hat.

It is in this cowboy dandy attire that Django blows Candyland to smithereens. While Stephen yells in protest that Candyland and, by extension, the social institution that it represents are indestructible ("You can't destroy Candyland! There's always gonna be a Candyland! Can't no nigger gunfighter kill all the white folks in the world!"), Django takes a few drags of his cigarette, removes Calvin's cigarette holder from his mouth, and uses it to light a long fuse running to a bundle of dynamite. He then walks out of the house, turns around to look back at the mansion as he dons a pair of silver-rimmed sunglasses, and waits for the fuse to blow. A shot of the big house exploding is followed by a wider view of Django standing invincibly in the middle of the frame with his hands on his hips as debris from the explosion burns around him. The movie's last shot shows Candyland being consumed by flames as Broomhilda and Django ride past the camera and off into the night.

In Nama's opinion, the movie's ending is a generic (in the pejorative sense) add-on to an otherwise original and compelling film. It "feels tacked on," Nama writes, "looks corny (the last thing I expect from a Tarantino film), and comes off more as parody than tribute."[27] Part of the reason that Nama dislikes the over-the-top spaghetti Western ending is surely due to the fact that it does not work within his overall paradigm for interpreting the movie. In his reading, *Django Unchained* is a Gothic horror film. As Nama admits, the last 30 or 40 minutes of the film do not fit within this critical framework. However, it is true also that, within the logic of the film narrative, there is no need for Django to blow up Candyland at the end of the movie. Heather Ashley Hayes and Gilbert Rodman make this point in a brilliant reading of the film appearing both in Speck's edited volume and as an article in *Jump Cut*. "Within the world of the film," Hayes and Rodman comment, "there was no need for Django to do anything about the 'big house' at all." However, the authors continue, "Django doesn't blow up Candyland because *he* needs to do so: he blows it up because *we* need him to do so": "*Django*'s real villain is not Stephen or Candie. It's not even a person at all. It's racism. And not racism as a scattered problem produced by isolated, individual bigots, but racism as a pervasive, unrelenting *structural* phenomenon. [...] If Django is going to triumph against *that* villain, he can't just kill off Candie and Stephen and then ride off into the night with Hildy: he needs to kill 'the big house' too."[28] In sum, the big house serves, in the movie, as an emblem of racism as an ideology and of slavery as an institution. Having spent the previous two and a half hours watching grisly depictions of the brutality and ugliness of that institution, the viewer yearns to see its destruction. In blowing up Candyland at the end of the movie, Django gives us our fantasy ending.

It is significant that Django accomplishes this final act of destruction while dressed like Calvin Candie, with the added accessories of the flashy cowboy hat and the dark glasses. Both visually and thematically, Django's burgundy cowboy ensemble is the culmination of a narrative that begins with him shackled in chains and proceeds to show his transformation, stage by stage, into a free black man in slave territory and an unstoppable force of righteous retribution. These two facets of the hero's emancipation, which correspond loosely to Django's burgundy suit, on the one hand, and his hat, sunglasses, and gun belt, on the other hand, are combined in the final sequence, when he demolishes Candyland while dressed like Monsieur Candie.

What better way to encode visually the black man's equality with white folks than to show him sporting the outfit of the film's most powerful and privileged white man while he blasts the symbol of white power and privilege to smithereens?

Wage Labor vs. Slave Labor

As the foregoing comments make obvious, *Django Unchained* engages directly with issues of race and racism in the United States. Predictably (and appropriately), the vast majority of the scholarship on the film examines those aspects of the movie. However, Django's revolt represents not only an assault on institutionalized racism. To the extent that chattel slavery in the antebellum South was both a codified system of racial discrimination and a legal form of capitalist exploitation, the enemy at the core of *Django Unchained* is both racism and capitalism. Tarantino suggests as much in his three-part interview with Gates: "I mean, the fourth-largest cotton plantation in Mississippi, which is what Candie's is—that's like owning Dole Pineapple or something today. It's a big, moneymaking, commercial enterprise."[29] Tarantino proposes here that Candyland, which, as indicated above, symbolizes systemic racism, is also emblematic of large-scale capitalist enterprise. The two phenomena are not always entirely dissociable, either in Tarantino's movieland or in the world outside the cinema. The intermeshing of these two phenomena leads African Americanist Keeanga-Yamahtta Taylor to argue that "any serious discussion about Black liberation has to take up not only a critique of capitalism, but also a credible strategy for ending it."[30] Taking the opposite approach, Marx famously argued a century and a half ago, in reference to the abolition of slavery in the United States, that "every independent workers' movement was paralysed as long as slavery disfigured a part of the republic."[31] Whether one sees, as Taylor does, the elimination of capitalism as a precondition for the emancipation of African

Americans or, on the contrary, one perceives, with Marx, the abolition of slavery as a necessary condition for a successful workers' movement, the narrative of a freed slave who burns the symbol of his oppression to the ground finds an integral place in a study of contemporary representations of the anti-capitalist struggle.

In one of the few scholarly essays on the film that address directly the issue of capitalism, William Brown argues that "slavery was part of a worldwide 'get-rich-quick' scheme."[32] He cites in this regard a letter written by Marx to Pavel Vasilyevich Annenko in 1846: "Direct slavery is the pivot of our industrialism today as much as machinery, credits, etc. Without slavery you have no cotton, without cotton you have no modern industry. It is slavery that has given value to the colonies; it is the colonies that created world trade; it is world trade that is the necessary condition for large-scale machine industry."[33] In sum, Marx concludes, slavery is "an economic category of the highest importance."[34] As Salome Lee, who cites these passages in a recent article, elucidates, "Marx was not by any means arguing for the necessity of slavery for social progress here."[35] On the contrary, Lee clarifies, Marx is advancing an argument against a system built on slavery.

Granted, as Marx readily recognizes, capitalism is by no means the only economic system in world history that has made use of slave labor. Marx brings into relief the long history of slavery by citing examples of ancient civilizations that thrived on forced unpaid labor. However, Marx comments, "in antiquity over-work becomes frightful only when the aim is to obtain exchange-value."[36] Once the sale of goods for profit comes to dominate over the local consumption of goods provided by slave labor, the relationship between the slave owner and the enslaved laborer qualitatively changes. At that point, David Harvey comments, glossing Marx, "any kind of human relationship that might have previously existed between master and slave will likely be destroyed."[37] Such, according to Marx, is what occurred in the United States over the course of the nineteenth century:

> The Negro labour in the southern states of the American Union preserved a moderately patriarchal character as long as production was chiefly directed to the satisfaction of immediate local requirements. But in proportion as the export of cotton became of vital interest to those states, the over-working of the Negro, and sometimes the consumption of his life in seven years of labour, became a factor in a calculated and calculating system. It was no longer a question of obtaining from him a certain quantity of useful products, but rather of the production of surplus-value itself.[38]

Under these conditions, in which the anticipated exchange value of a product takes precedence over its immediate use value, the slave loses whatever vestiges of humanity she might have retained in previous socioeconomic configurations. Under the pressure of capitalist expansion, the slave owner's objective becomes maximum wealth extraction from the labor of the slave, who is reduced, in the process, to the status of an organic machine. In the terms of Marx's distinction between "constant capital" (which includes capital invested in machinery, raw materials, and so forth) and "variable capital" (which refers to money paid to workers in the form of wages), the slave represents a living form of "constant capital."

This distinction between "constant capital" and "variable capital" brings into relief a fundamental difference between slave labor and wage labor. Whereas the slave receives no compensation for her work, the wage laborer does. Moreover, the worker is not forced to work in the same way that a slave is. Marx insists on this point in his 1846 letter to Annenko, where he distinguishes between "indirect slavery, the slavery of the proletariat," and "direct slavery, the slavery of Blacks in Surinam, in Brazil, in the southern states of North America."[39] However, although the wage laborer is free to leave her master at any time, she cannot opt out of the capitalist system altogether without completely withdrawing from society. She is not enslaved to any particular capitalist but, rather, to the capitalist system as a whole. With a final fillip, although the worker is "free" to sell her labor power on the open market, she forfeits her freedom in the exchange. As David Graeber writes: "A wage-labor contract is, ostensibly, a free contract between equals—but an agreement between equals in which both agree that once one of them punches the time clock, they won't be equals any more."[40] The scenario described here compels Graeber to conclude that "there is, and has always been, a curious affinity between wage labor and slavery": "whether you've been sold or you've simply rented yourself out, the moment money changes hands, [...] all that's important is that you are capable of understanding orders and doing what you're told."[41]

With the seemingly inexorable colonization of the world's remaining non-capitalist enclaves, the opportunities that existed in the past to "opt out" of the system proportionally diminish. The recent scholarly interest in the "enclosure of the commons" is, in part, a result of this diminution. The expression refers to the mass privatization of hitherto common lands that took place in sixteenth-century England, when communal plots of land were literally "enclosed" by fences, leaving farmers little choice but to work as wage laborers for the new class of landowners. The contemporary "enclosure of the commons" is a similar phenomenon, taking place now on a global scale. It has opened up new terrains for resource extraction around the world while simultaneously creating a vast, international labor market. Together with technological innovations that have improved efficiency and made human labor increasingly superfluous, the creation of this global labor market (an extension, on an international scale, of the population mass that Marx, following

Friedrich Engels, called capital's "reserve army of labour"[42]) has resulted in widespread unemployment and underemployment in the formerly industrialized countries, on the one hand, and the concomitant suppression of wages around the world, including in the so-called "developing world," on the other hand. In short, it has culminated in mass poverty on an international scale while permitting a small handful of capitalist entrepreneurs to increase astronomically their share of the world's wealth. Rather than turning former Third World countries into First World countries, its effect has been the gradual conversion of virtually the whole world into a vast Third World.

Marx foresaw this development 150 years ago. In the climactic chapter of *Capital* entitled "The General Law of Capitalist Accumulation," Marx famously claimed:

> The greater the social wealth, the functioning capital, the extent and energy of its growth, and therefore also the greater the absolute mass of the proletariat and the productivity of its labour, the greater is the industrial reserve army. [...] But the greater this reserve army in proportion to the active labour-army, the greater is the mass of a consolidated surplus population, whose misery is in inverse ratio to the amount of torture it has to undergo in the form of labour. The more extensive, finally, the pauperized sections of the working class and the industrial reserve army, the greater is official pauperism. *This is the absolute general law of capitalist accumulation.*[43]

This is the notorious theory of immiseration, which Marx summarizes in the form: "in proportion as capital accumulates, the situation of the worker [...] must grow worse."[44] As Jameson comments in his recent book on *Capital*, this immiseration theory "was the object of much mockery during the affluent post-war 1950s and 1960s. It is today no longer a joking matter."[45]

Following Ernest Mandel, who claims, in his introduction to the Penguin edition of *Capital*, that contemporary capitalism is much closer to the model described by Marx than was the capitalism of Marx's day, Jameson argues that the economic processes described by Marx 150 years ago anticipate developments that had not yet taken place in Marx's time.[46] Rather than being outdated or obsolete in the twenty-first century, Jameson argues, Marx's theory was ahead of its time in the nineteenth. It pertains more to our world than to Marx's. *Capital* is, in sum, arguably more relevant now than it ever was. It analyzes an "abstract" form of capitalism that took "concrete" form only in the latter decades of the twentieth century. Marx's theoretical fiction of capital working optimally, according to its internal logic, has become our empirical global reality.

The Insurrection to Come

Whereas Marx's theory of immiseration was 150 years ahead of its time, his conception of revolutionary social change was not. If Marx is correct—as history has shown him to be—that, unhindered, capitalism would create an ever-more powerful class of wealthy capitalists at one pole and untold misery at the opposite pole, his theory of class struggle (penned, it is true, some 2 decades before *Capital*, at a time when proletarian revolution seemed imminent) does not account for this tendency. On the contrary, the Marxian theory of revolution, as developed in conjunction with Engels in the 1848 *Communist Manifesto*, relies on a conception of a traditional working class organizing on the floors of factories in urban centers. "Masses of labourers, crowded into the factory, are organised like soldiers," the authors claim.[47] "With the development of industry," they assert, "the proletariat not only increases in number; it becomes concentrated in greater masses, its strength grows, and it feels that strength more."[48] Needless to say, in the early twenty-first century, neither the strength of the working class nor its feeling of empowerment is on the rise. On the contrary, both the traditional working class and working-class consciousness are arguably at their lowest ebb since Marx and Engels wrote their manifesto in the 1840s. This decline of working-class power has crippling repercussions for the prospective social revolution that Marx and Engels envision. For if, as they argue, "of all the classes that stand face to face with the bourgeoisie today, the proletariat alone is a really revolutionary class," this sole revolutionary agent is now in precipitous decline.[49]

By isolating the proletariat as the uniquely positioned agent of revolutionary change, Marx and Engels discount not only the revolutionary potential of the peasantry (a group that has seen an even sharper demographic decline than that of the traditional urban working class); they also relegate to the margins of history the rapidly growing ranks of the non-working abject poor. The latter group, which Marx and Engels give the unflattering name of the *lumpenproletariat*—"that passively rotting mass thrown off by the lowest layers of the old society," in the authors' derisive words—is quickly becoming the largest social class in the world.[50]

Marx and Engels are not alone in dismissing the revolutionary potential of the lumpenproletariat. In *Wages of Rebellion*, Chris Hedges compiles a mini-dossier of left-wing social thinkers, beginning with Marx and Engels, who argue, each in his or her own way, that "it is never the poor [...] who make revolutions."[51] Hedges approvingly cites in this regard historian Crane Brinton: "The idea that the very oppressed and poor are important as initiating and maintaining revolution is a bourgeois one."[52] Rather than coming from the ranks of the poor, Hedges argues, revolutions spring from "a disenfranchised middle class and alienated members of the ruling class."[53]

In direct opposition to this argument, David Harvey argues, in *Seventeen Contradictions and the End of Capitalism*, that in the twenty-first century, revolution is more likely to come from the swelling ranks of the destitute poor than from discontented members of the privileged and semi-privileged classes. The figure to whom Harvey turns in order to elaborate what such a revolution might look like is Frantz Fanon, the revolutionary anti-colonialist whose 1961 *The Wretched of the Earth* argues for the violent overthrow of colonialism. Although, as Harvey acknowledges, Fanon's analysis is specific to the anti-colonial struggles of the twentieth century, it "illustrates the sorts of issues that arise in any liberation struggle, including those between capital and labour."[54] Following a similar train of thought, post-colonial theorist Homi Bhabha forcefully forges a link between the colonialism of yesteryear and contemporary global capitalism. As Bhabha writes in his foreword to the 2004 edition of Fanon's book: "*The Wretched of the Earth* does indeed allow us to look well beyond the immediacies of its anticolonial context—the Algerian war of independence and the African continent—toward a critique of the configurations of contemporary globalization."[55] "With a few exceptions," Bhabha argues, "the cartography of the global south follows the contours of the Third World."[56]

Fanon's conception of colonialism is particularly pertinent to thinking about the slave narrative presented in *Django Unchained* given the superimposition of class onto race that Fanon perceived in the colonial system: "In the colonies the economic infrastructure is also a superstructure," he famously proclaimed. "The cause is effect: You are rich because you are white, you are white because you are rich."[57] Although Fanon's pronouncement was too categorical to be taken as an absolute truth at his time, and is even less categorically true today, as the growing number of poor white people around the world can attest, there was, and still is, a grain of truth to it. This kernel of truth becomes apparent if we look at the other side of racial and class divides in the context of the contemporary US. Rather than stating, as Fanon does, that "you are rich because you are white," if one proposed instead that "you are poor because you are black," the formula would be more immediately relevant in the context of the twenty-first-century United States. Although it is no longer true—if it ever was, even in the colonies—that being white guaranteed one's wealth, being black does go a long way, in the present-day US, to ensuring one's poverty. Among racial and ethnic groups in the United States, African Americans currently have the highest poverty rate, 27.4 percent (a ratio of more than one to four), as compared to whites at 9.9 percent (a ratio of less than one to ten).[58]

The present inequality between African Americans and European Americans can be traced to specific policy decisions made by US presidential administrations during the post-civil rights years. An early step in this direction was President Nixon's notorious "drug war" of the early 1970s. A surprisingly candid after-the-fact admission by John Ehrlichman, Nixon's senior adviser (now best known for his role in the Watergate break-in), divulges that the real enemies in this ill-fated drug war were "the antiwar left [a reference to protestors against the Vietnam War] and black people": "We knew we couldn't make it illegal to be either against the war or black, but by getting the public to associate the hippies with marijuana and blacks with heroin, and then criminalizing both heavily, we could disrupt those communities. We could arrest their leaders, raid their homes, break up their meetings, and vilify them night after night on the evening news. Did we know we were lying about the drugs? Of course we did."[59]

As Michelle Alexander's *The New Jim Crow: Mass Incarceration in the Age of Colorblindness* demonstrates, Ronald Reagan's renewal of the war on drugs in 1982 follows a similar logic. The upshot of Reagan's war on drugs is extraordinary: the United States now has by far the highest rate of incarceration in the world. As Alexander argues, "The racial dimension of mass incarceration is its most striking feature. No other country in the world imprisons so many of its racial or ethnic minorities." As a point of comparison, Alexander notes that the United States imprisons "a larger percentage of its black population than South Africa did at the height of apartheid."[60] Moreover, the mass incarcerations that began under Reagan have resulted not only in the loss of the inmates' freedom and, with it, their civil rights. These incarcerations also quite literally convert people into human slaves. Although slavery has been illegal for free citizens in the United States for more than a century and a half, it is legal to enslave convicted criminals. This is a capitalist's dream come true, especially as the number of people behind bars increases with each passing decade. An extraordinarily large number of multinational corporations—including Whole Foods, McDonald's, Wal-Mart, Victoria's Secret, and dozens of others—benefit from this vast supply of slave labor.[61]

However, the assault on people of color orchestrated by the Reagan administration goes far beyond the arrest, conviction, and incarceration of non-whites for drug-related crimes. A 1981 interview with Lee Atwater, a strategic adviser in the Reagan White House, reveals that an innocuous sounding expression like "tax cuts" is a dog-whistle term not only for class warfare (which we already knew), but for a race war as well. In this interview, Atwater divulges with shocking forthrightness and in unabashedly racist language that "cutting taxes" is code for subjugating African Americans.[62] In sum, a series of measures put into place during the post-civil rights years have had the intended effect of creating a racially defined "internal Third World" in the core of the First World.

Fanon's proposed course of action in the face of such a two-tiered system is uncompromising: "To destroy the colonial world means nothing less than demolishing the colonist's sector, burying it deep within the earth or banishing it from the territory."[63] In short, he proposes a course of action not unlike the one that Django undertakes in Tarantino's film, when the freewheeling cowboy blows Candyland to smithereens in the movie's final scene. Here Stephen's protestations as Django prepares to blow Candyland to bits take on their full significance. When Stephen affirms that Candyland, by which he means the institution of slavery that the plantation represents, is indestructible ("There's always gonna be a Candyland!"), he gives voice to the prevailing neoliberal *doxa* that the reign of unbridled global capital is here to stay. Seeing the freed slave accomplish the "impossible" task of demolishing the film's physical embodiment of this allegedly indestructible system—and knowing that, in the years following the film's diegetic conclusion in 1859, that system was indeed destroyed—enables the viewer to imagine that the seemingly unassailable system of contemporary global capitalism may too be vulnerable to attack.

Chapter 5

Negations of the Negation: *Elysium* and *Snowpiercer*

This last chapter examines two recent science-fiction films that explicitly present themselves as allegories of the end of capitalism. Extrapolating from the growing divide between rich and poor, Neill Blomkamp's *Elysium* and Bong Joon-ho's *Snowpiercer* (both 2013) depict a rigorous segregation of the wealthy elite from the teeming masses of the destitute. While *Elysium* presents a future in which the upper class has abandoned the polluted and overpopulated Earth and moved onto the luxury space station of Elysium, in *Snowpiercer* the abject poor live at the back of a massive locomotive—the "Snowpiercer" of the film's title—while the idle rich live in comfort and security in the first-class cars at the front of the train. However, although they start from a common premise, the two films propose dissimilar solutions to the social problem that they depict. Whereas *Elysium* imagines appropriating the global capitalist apparatus and making it work for the benefit of all humanity, *Snowpiercer* allegorizes the violent destruction of the means as well as the relations of capitalist production. The two movies present in this way two very different visions of the process that Karl Marx called "the negation of the negation." While one film envisions a post-capitalist future that builds on and benefits from the progress that capitalism has made, the other imagines the wholesale demolition of the capitalist machine.

This chapter explores Blomkamp's and Bong's different representations of class difference and class struggle, and the filmmakers' contrasting hypothetical resolutions to the fundamental contradiction they depict. It begins with an examination of the two social spaces portrayed in Blomkamp's

Elysium: the luxury residential satellite, on the one hand, and the sprawling slums of a future Los Angeles, on the other. Giving graphic visual form to socio-spatial divisions between the rich and the poor that authors such as cultural theorist Peter Sloterdijk, sociologist Saskia Sassen, and urban historian Mike Davis present in their writings on the geographies of capitalism, *Elysium*, set in the year 2154, pushes current class differences to their logical conclusion, exaggerating only by a matter of degree a phenomenon well underway in the early twenty-first century. The film has the additional merit of presenting the swathe of humanity living on Earth as a hodgepodge of unemployed, precariously employed, and illegally employed workers and former workers alongside an anonymous mass of the structurally unemployable. Each of these groups has been growing at an alarming rate in recent decades, making the movie all too relevant in the present context. What unites members of these different social groups, in the film, is also eminently topical. What brings together the working poor, the pauperized, and the human traffickers and gunrunners of *Elysium* is their shared need for access to healthcare. When, at the end of the film, all inhabitants of Earth are declared citizens of Elysium and billions of slum dwellers prepare to board spacecrafts taking them to the state-of-the-art medical facilities on the space station, we glimpse a utopian vision of free comprehensive universal healthcare for everyone on Earth, regardless of employment status.

Unlike the denizens of Blomkamp's Los Angeles, the inhabitants of the rear cars of Snowpiercer are a socially homogeneous (although racially diverse) group. From the first shot of the grime-covered beings huddled at the back of the train, we are given to understand that they represent the lowest stratum of society: those stigmatized by Marx and Engels as "lumpens." The film narrates the transformation of this notoriously reactionary subclass into a revolutionary army, allegorizing the creation of a collective revolutionary subject from those on the bottom rung of the social ladder, rather than one composed of a vanguard of the working class. Giving cartoon-like narrative and audio-visual form to debates that have animated Marxist-Leninist and anarchist traditions for more than a century, the film shows members of this group debating whether or not now is the right time to act, deciding in the blink of an eye to risk everything in an assault on their oppressors, and then fighting their way progressively from the back to the front of the train, all the way to the engine room. However, rather than keeping the engine running, the insurgents derail the train, bringing the machine to a crashing halt. The chapter concludes with an examination of the ways that this train wreck at the end of *Snowpiercer* allegorizes the demise of capitalism, and the ambiguous hope that the film holds for survivors of the crash.

Global Slums and the International Gated Community

Elysium introduces its principal metaphor for class division from its opening images. The movie begins with a series of helicopter shots taking us from a shantytown to a massive trash dump on the outskirts of a city, and from there to aerial views of a sprawling *favela*, a distressed urban ghetto, and finally a set of crumbling skyscrapers at the heart of a downtown vaguely resembling that of present-day Los Angeles. The scene then cuts to a view of Earth from outer space, the camera holding steady for a few seconds and then panning to a torus-shaped space station hovering at the edge of the Earth's atmosphere. Replicating the movement of the film's opening shots, the camera then glides over a continuous tract of land running along the inner rim of the satellite's wheel-like structure. As the camera soars over this 2-kilometer-wide strip of manicured lawn, it reveals stately mansions nestled among rolling hills, interspersed with manmade lakes and clusters of shopping malls, sports centers, and futuristic office buildings. In the space of about a minute and a half, the film has brought into stark relief two diametrically opposed social spaces. Whereas Earth is presented as an overpopulated urban wasteland, Elysium is the upscale suburban gated community of the future. One is as safe, secure, and sedate as the other is dilapidated and decrepit.

In *Trouble in Paradise*, Slavoj Žižek assimilates *Elysium*'s orbital space habitat to the Crystal Palace project at the heart of Peter Sloterdijk's *In the World Interior of Capital* (2005).[1] Built originally in London's Hyde Park for the 1851 Great Exhibition, the cast-iron and plate-glass Crystal Palace covered roughly a million square feet of surface area. Its clear walls and ceilings reached an interior height of 128 feet, creating an immersive environment with an invisible shell protecting the palace's interior space from the world outside. Functioning in Sloterdijk's interpretation as a metaphor for nascent global capitalism, the palatial glasshouse "captured the inevitable exclusivity of globalization as the construction and expansion of a world interior whose boundaries are invisible yet virtually insurmountable from without."[2] This metaphorical "capitalist world palace," as Sloterdijk calls it, currently harbors roughly 30 percent of the world's population.[3] Its boundaries may expand and contract over time, integrating new citizens while "[rejecting] former dwellers" and "[threatening] many of the spatially included with social exclusion," but "it would be a misinterpretation," Sloterdijk argues, "to demand that the palace contain 'mankind' in its full numbers."[4] On the contrary, he insists, "Exclusivity is inherent to the crystal palace project as such."[5] Modeled after a hothouse rather than an agora, an open-air market, or a residential building, this paradigmatic capitalist structure creates "a domestically organized and artificially climatized inner space" that shelters and protects its privileged inhabitants while keeping the world's have-nots firmly locked out.[6]

The idea of representing the Crystal Palace of the future as a doughnut-shaped orbital space habitat complete with upscale neighborhoods built around artificial lakes may seem absurd, but the design for Elysium is in fact based on a model created by an organization no less reputable than the National Aeronautics and Space Administration (NASA), the US government's civilian space program.[7] Unveiled at NASA's 1975 Summer Study seminar at Stanford University, plans for the so-called Stanford Torus present a ring-shaped rotating space station capable of housing up to 140,000 permanent residents. Blomkamp's orbital habitat, based on drawings by concept artist Syd Mead, bears remarkable similarity to renderings of the Stanford Torus. The layout of a wheel-shaped satellite with six "spokes" (reduced to five in *Elysium*), the conglomerations of individual housing units built onto verdant rolling hills, the sculpted bodies of water, and even the glimmering recreation centers and futuristic office buildings that dot the landscape of Elysium appear in NASA's 1975 sketches of the torus.

What Blomkamp and production designer Phil Ivey add to the Stanford Torus is opulence and tackiness. Rather than a floating EPCOT Center, the filmmaker wanted Elysium to look "more like Beverly Hills from the air, or Bel Air,"[8] a reference to regions in Los Angeles' Westside that, according to urban historian Mike Davis, contain "one of the largest concentrations of affluence on the planet."[9] This vision of "Bel Air in space" accounts for the extravagance of the houses on Elysium.[10] In contrast to the relatively uniform cubical dwellings found in NASA's designs, Blomkamp's space station contains a variety of housing styles, "from your faux Tuscan," Phil Ivey specifies, "through to ultramodern styles."[11] *Elysium* would have us envision a future in which the slums of LA have overrun even such enclaves of safety and security as Bel Air and Beverly Hills. The wealthy elite have therefore abandoned their Earth-bound gated communities and taken up residence on a floating space station situated some 100 kilometers above the Earth's surface, replicating their erstwhile lifestyle, including their glass and stucco mansions, on the space habitat.

One of the noteworthy features of this orbital habitat is its multiculturalism. Although the majority of Elysium's residents are white, inhabitants include people of sub-Saharan African, East Asian, and South Asian descent. This racial diversity reflects a class division that traverses traditional regional and cultural communities, opposing an international elite to a global population of slum dwellers. It thereby bears witness, in its own way, to what sociologist Saskia Sassen calls "the fact of growing cross-border interactions among [the] increasingly global elites" that inhabit the world's gated communities.[12] In Sassen's view, such cross-border interactions are one of the hallmarks of contemporary capitalism. The "geographies of centrality that connect the power centres of the world," as she calls them, tend increasingly to "cut across the old North-South divide," creating an international capitalist class that transcends regional boundaries.[13] In *Beyond Gated Communities* — a title referring to the larger global trend that urban gating represents in microcosmic form — Samer Bagaeen and Ola Uduku speak in this regard of "the growing nation of residents in various forms of gated communities across the globe."[14] The formulation is telling. This international class of the wealthy and privileged form a "nation" unto themselves, Bagaeen and Uduku suggest, regardless of the particular nation-state in which the individuals happen to reside. An international space station of a new sort, Elysium gives graphic visual form to such a state of affairs. Rather than situating the suburban paradise of the future in a specific national or cultural context, Blomkamp envisions an extraterrestrial gated community that transcends ethnographic as well as regional divisions.

The living conditions of those excluded from the international Crystal Palace are lavishly detailed in Blomkamp's film. From our first glimpse inside the protagonist's prison cell-like cubicle to the street-level shots of his *favela*, the movie communicates with crystalline clarity the living standards of the have-nots of the future. As Max Da Costa (Matt Damon) walks from his ramshackle 10-by-20-foot brick house past the heaps of recycled building materials piled up in his front yard to the bus stop at the bottom of the hill, he traverses a densely populated neighborhood where scavengers and beggars mingle with swarms of people standing around chatting or wandering on the unpaved thoroughfare. Trash is strewn everywhere; chickens run loose in the streets; a chained dog barks from behind a dilapidated wooden enclosure; piles of rubble litter the roadway; improvised structures of corrugated iron and scrap lumber stand side-by-side with makeshift cinderblock domiciles, many of them without windowpanes, a door, or a roof. The scene as a whole gives stark visual form to the type of metropolis described by Mike Davis in *Planet of Slums*:

> The cities of the future, rather than being made out of glass and steel as envisioned by earlier generations of urbanists, are instead largely constructed out of crude brick, straw, recycled plastic, cement blocks, and scrap wood. Instead of cities of light soaring toward heaven, much of the twenty-first-century urban world squats in squalor, surrounded by pollution, excrement, and decay.[15]

One of Blomkamp's strokes of genius is his decision to depict the sprawling urban ghetto of twenty-second-century LA by filming on location in the streets of present-day Mexico City. The bombed-out buildings that form the Los Angeles skyline are computer-generated images, and Ivey's art department "added another layer of filth" to the filming location by incorporating such details as graffiti, wrecked cars, and animals roaming the streets,[16] but if the Los Angeles of the future bears an uncanny resemblance to the Mexico of the present, it is because it is. The massive *favela* of the next century's Hollywood Hills, where Max

Da Costa lives in 2154, is the mega-slum of today's Neza, on the eastern edge of Mexico City. The future is now, the film implies, even if it is not necessarily "here" in Los Angeles. To glean the future slums of the First World, the movie suggests, one need only abstract from the contemporary cities of the former Third World.

The decision to set the film in LA, as opposed to a city like Mexico (or Rio de Janeiro, where Blomkamp originally intended to both set and shoot the movie), merits comment. Blomkamp gives two explanations for this decision. On the one hand, he thought that First World audiences would be able to "relate" more to a film set in what is currently an affluent Western city. On the other hand, he states in regard to his dystopian vision of the future La-La Land, "in my personal set of beliefs and predictions, this is where LA is going. [...] And to a certain extent, it's where the First World is going, as well."[17] If the first explanation pertains primarily to marketing, the second communicates a socio-historical vision akin to the one that undergirds Mike Davis' *City of Quartz: Excavating the Future in Los Angeles*. As its subtitle suggests, Davis' book proposes not to excavate the future *of* LA, but *in* or *from* it. "As California goes, so goes the nation," according to a popular adage. What Blomkamp and Davis suggest is: as the state's most populated city goes, so goes the advanced capitalist world more generally.

Simultaneously "the First World capital of homelessness" and home to one of the densest concentrations of wealth on the planet, Los Angeles — a city which, in Davis' book, occasionally functions as "a stand-in for capitalism in general" — is characterized by extremes of wealth inequality.[18] Also characteristic of the city are the clear demarcation lines separating one socioeconomic demographic from another. Social exclusion is paramount in this Southern Californian Crystal Palace, where a massive enclosure of the commons has led to a wholesale privatization of previously public space: "In Los Angeles, once-upon-a-time a demi-paradise of free beaches, luxurious parks, and 'cruising strips,' genuinely democratic space is all but extinct. The Oz-like archipelago of Westside pleasure domes—a continuum of tony malls, arts centers and gourmet strips—is reciprocally dependent upon the social imprisonment of the third-world service proletariat who live in increasingly repressive ghettos and barrios."[19] A socio-historical urban street map that simultaneously provides a fascinating "cognitive map" of contemporary capitalism, Davis' book on LA details a city in which extreme wealth inequality and apartheid-like segregation go hand in hand.

Blomkamp's apocalyptic future reflects this dystopian present. His fictional twenty-second-century world embellishes ongoing developments in our world, bringing them into sharp relief so that we might see them more clearly. If, as Fredric Jameson proposes in *Archaeologies of the Future*, the "deepest subject" of science fiction is not "the attempt to imagine unimaginable futures" but, rather, "our own historical present," *Elysium* is an exemplary sci-fi film.[20]

Industrial-Labor Relations

It is significant that in this film about class relations, the first line uttered by the protagonist pertains to his employment status. As Max Da Costa walks in his factory coveralls from his house to the bus stop, a couple of beer drinking neighbors mock him for going to work. "That's real funny. I have a job," he mutters in response. At this early moment in the film we do not yet realize that the beer drinkers are right to ridicule the slavish Da Costa, whose job entails fabricating the police droids that keep the Angelinos in their place through gratuitous harassment and the constant threat of violence. Indeed, this scene of Max heading off to work culminates in his being assaulted by a pair of law-enforcement droids that throw him to the ground and beat him, breaking his arm in the process, because he responded to their street interrogation with a joke. The irony is therefore not lost when, 5 minutes later, we see the proud employee assembling robots of the same sort in a factory on the other side of town. Max's job consists of fabricating the machines that repress people like him.

The protagonist's job building police robots contributes to the misery of life on Earth in a second, more generalizable way as well. As Paul Verhoeven's *RoboCop* dramatized more than 3 decades ago, the replacement of police officers by combat droids represents one battle in a larger class war between capital and labor.[21] In his insightful chapter on technology, work, and human disposability in *Seventeen Contradictions and the End of Capitalism*, David Harvey explains why this is so: "Robots do not [...] complain, answer back, sue, get sick, go slow, lose concentration, go on strike, demand more wages, worry about work conditions, want tea breaks or simply refuse to show up."[22] Reminding us that technological innovation has long been "a crucial weapon in class struggle," Harvey shows how the organic composition of capital has shifted dramatically in recent decades from human resources to technological resources, rendering social labor redundant in one sector after another as innovative new machines do more and more of the work formerly done by human beings. The result has been increased productivity and efficiency on the one hand and mass unemployment on the other. Surveying recent trends and evaluating future prospects, Harvey's conclusion anticipates a scenario akin to the one depicted in *Elysium*: "massive surpluses of potentially restive redundant populations."[23]

That surplus population, represented in the film by the throngs of people milling about the city streets, constitutes a huge industrial reserve army of unemployed but potentially employable workers. As this labor reserve grows, individual workers become increasingly expendable, leading to their decreased bargaining power and perforce, to a decline in their real wages, a deterioration of their working conditions, an erosion of their rights, and their increased precariousness. Such is the situation at Armadyne, the armaments manufactory where Max Da Costa works.

We can glean the state of industrial-labor relations at Armadyne from the first exchange between Max and his foreman. Seeing Max arrive late for work with a cast on his arm, his supervisor tells him that he cannot work in that state. When Max protests that he can do his job with a broken arm, the foreman gives the OK, informing the laborer that he is nonetheless going to dock Da Costa half a day's pay and justifying this decision on the grounds that Max is "lucky to have this job." Although the foreman does not refer explicitly here to the multitude of unemployed people that could work in Da Costa's place, the existence of such an industrial reserve army subtends his rationale.

The foreman's initial concern when he sees Max's broken arm appears to be safety. As the droning loudspeaker periodically reminds workers on the shop floor, "Safety is our priority" at Armadyne. The second scene set in the assembly plant belies this concern. Da Costa's specific task in the production process is bolting steel plates onto finished torso sections and then placing the torsos into a kiln that treats the finished articles with radiation. In the second factory scene, the kiln door jams, bringing production to a halt. Seeing that the pallet inside the chamber is preventing the door from closing, the foreman instructs Max to go in and dislodge the pinched pallet. When Max refuses, the supervisor gives him an ultimatum: "Look, either you go in there right now or I'll find someone who will, and you can clean out your locker." Max then reluctantly enters the kiln and extricates the pallet, enabling the door to close automatically with him trapped inside the chamber. The automated treatment process then continues, zapping Max with a lethal dose of radiation. Lest we think that this sort of toxic exposure is a rare occurrence at Armadyne, Max's subsequent explanation of what transpired clearly suggests that it is not. When his friend Julio (Diego Luna) asks him what happened, Max explains: "I took a full dose, man. I got a full dose." No further details are necessary for Julio to understand immediately what occurred. Moreover, in order to make sure that we grasp management's position on workplace accidents of this sort, Blomkamp has Armadyne CEO John Carlyle (William Fichtner) express his concern in unequivocal terms. Peering at Max through a window of the first aid room, the CEO asks: "Does his skin fall off or something? I don't want to replace the bedding. Just get him out." Carlyle is greatly concerned about the accident, but the subject of his concern is the interruption of the production schedule (and secondarily, as suggested here, the potential soiling of bed sheets), not the employee's condition.

CEO Carlyle's response to the news of Da Costa's radiation poisoning may be caricatural, but it is not completely fanciful. It approximates in tenor if not in tone industry leaders' responses to numerous workplace disasters, from the 2005 Spectrum garment factory collapse to the Tazreen Fashion factory fire in 2012. On the one hand, these responses tend to parody the reaction of *Casablanca*'s Captain Renault when he "discovers" that there is gambling in Rick's Café. Industry leaders are shocked — shocked — to find that their suppliers were forcing employees to work in unsafe conditions. Yet, on the other hand, these captains of industry resist committing to legally binding legislation that would prevent such workplace disasters from occurring in the future. Consequently, according to a 2015 report issued by the NYU Stern Center for Business and Human Rights, only eight of the 3425 factories inspected following the catastrophic 2013 Rana Plaza collapse had "remedied violations enough to pass a final inspection," even though the facilities were still producing goods for a vast array of multinational retailers.[24] *Elysium*'s Carlyle might be a caricature of the profit-driven CEO, but he is one drawn from life.

The scene that initially introduces Carlyle, when we see him overseeing production from his office overlooking the factory floor while simultaneously conducting an online board meeting with senior executives, clarifies his position and his motives. "If we don't have a clear path to upside," one of the board members warns the CEO, "our investors are going to start losing a lot of confidence." "What do you think I've been doing down here on Earth?" Carlyle rhetorically asks in response. "I am doing everything possible to restore profitability to this company." This brief exchange reveals a great deal not just about Carlyle's particular predicament but also about corporate capitalism in general.

First, as Joel Bakan demonstrates in *The Corporation*, senior executives at publicly traded corporations have one and only one mandate: to increase shareholder value. Examining the precedent-setting court cases that have established the legal definition of the corporation as an institution, Bakan concludes that the law "compels executives to prioritize the interests of their companies and shareholders above all others and forbids them from being socially responsible."[25] Injurious and unethical activity is fine provided that it does not adversely affect the company's profitability; charitable or socially responsible actions, by contrast, are *illegal* unless they contribute directly or indirectly to maximizing returns to shareholders. As repugnant as Carlyle's response to Da Costa's mishap may be, it is consistent with his legally mandated role as chief executive officer of a public corporation.

Second, Carlyle's exchange with the board member reveals that Armadyne is losing rather than making money. Even while benefiting from the existence of a fathomless disposable workforce, the company is not turning a profit. Although no explanation is given in the film for this negative balance sheet, it conjures the notorious "falling rate of profit" hypothesized by Marx. Variously referred to by Marx as a "law," a "tendency," and a "law of a tendency," the falling-profits theory postulates that technological innovations, while profitable in an initial stage to the companies that first implement them, reduce aggregate corporate profits in the long term.[26] As companies emulate their rivals, implementing new technologies that enable them to remain competitive, the ratio of constant capital (money invested in physical resources as well as raw materials) to variable capital (money paid to workers in the form of wages) increases across entire sectors. With this increase, the value (measured by the quantity of human labor power concentrated in the commodity) of each article falls, producing in turn a concomitant decrease in the rate of surplus value in relation to the total capital invested. The "gradual growth in the constant capital, in relation to the variable," must therefore, in Marx's view, "necessarily result in a *gradual fall in the general rate of profit.*"[27] While lucrative from a micro-economic perspective in the short term, technological innovation, which "is always towards savings in socially necessary labour time," is disastrous to the system as whole in the long term.[28]

This tendency for profits to fall, which Marx calls at one point "the most important law of modern political economy,"[29] is subject to half a dozen countervailing tendencies, making this "law" far less ironclad than such an assertion would suggest.[30] The theory has been the subject of much controversy among both Marxists and non-Marxists.[31] One of its merits in our context here is that it accounts for falling profits even in an environment, such as the one depicted in *Elysium*, where the existence of a massive industrial reserve army enables the capitalist class to keep labor costs to a minimum. One might think that the tendential redundancy of human labor and the wage suppression that it permits—twin phenomena unfolding on an unprecedented global scale in the twenty-first century—would enable capitalists to reap untold profits on an ongoing basis. Marx's theory of falling profits explains why this may not be the case. Judging from the one capitalist corporation depicted in the film, capitalism is in crisis in *Elysium*, before or beyond the potential for a popular uprising on the part of a downtrodden population of slum dwellers.

In sum, *Elysium* combines two of Marx's great theories for the end of capitalism. On the one hand, it depicts the tension between a capitalist elite that owns the means of production and the multitude of working poor and unemployed that form capital's workforce and its "industrial reserve army." According to "the historical tendency of capitalist accumulation" described in volume 1 of *Capital*, this contradiction is destined to intensify rather than subside over time. If capitalism follows its inner logic (which it certainly has been doing over the past few decades), capital will become increasingly concentrated in the hands of an ever-smaller number of capitalist magnates while, at the same time, "the mass of misery, oppression, slavery, degradation and exploitation grows."[32] However, Marx insists, as this contradiction becomes increasingly pronounced over time, "there also grows the revolt of the working class."[33] This growing unrest leads to the famous "negation of the negation," which spectacularly culminates, in chapter 32 of *Capital*, in the "bursting asunder" of the capitalist integument: "The centralization of the means of production and the socialization of labour reach a point at which they become incompatible with their capitalist integument. This integument is burst asunder. The knell of capitalist property sounds. The expropriators are expropriated."[34] According to this first scenario, what the capitalist class ultimately produces in its single-minded pursuit of profit are, in Marx's resonant formulation, "its own grave diggers."[35]

On the other hand, the movie simultaneously conjures the dead-end that capitalism reaches when "individual capitalists, acting in their own self-interest under the social relations of capitalist production and exchange, generate a technological mix that threatens further accumulation, destroys the potentiality for balanced growth and puts the reproduction of the capitalist class as a whole in jeopardy."[36] Summoning by turns the class war between capital and labor and the law of falling profits, *Elysium* beckons us to contemplate both the future of capitalism and its prospective demise from two complementary perspectives.

Expropriating the Expropriators

Of these two scenarios, it is the narrative of class antagonism that drives the plot. Following Max's radiation exposure, which is destined to kill him within 5 days' time, he seeks out two characters that might be able to help him: Frey (Alice Braga), his childhood sweetheart and abiding love interest, who works as a nurse in an overcrowded and underfunded inner-city hospital, and Spider (Wagner Moura), the leader of an LA street gang. Whereas Frey can offer Max nothing more than palliative care, Spider runs a human trafficking operation that transports sick people to Elysium, where every house is equipped with a medical bay that can scan the human body and repair anomalies it detects. The fee that Spider charges for his service is exorbitant, and the trip is extremely hazardous, but business is booming. Invoking the human smuggling operations that thrive on capitalism's uneven global development, Spider's organization profits from the plight of vulnerable populations that have no legal means to enter the Crystal Palace.

Spider agrees to transport Max to Elysium if, in exchange, Max accepts a dangerous mission entailing the transfer of data from an Elysian's brain to his own. The mark, by Da Costa's choice, is Armadyne CEO Carlyle, who, unbeknownst to his attackers, has uploaded an Elysium system reboot into his brain with the aim of striking a business deal with Elysian Defense Secretary Delacourt (Jodie Foster). When Spider receives the stolen data, he realizes that he has the power to modify the computer program that functions as the de facto Constitution of Elysium. With a single keystroke, he declares all of Earth's inhabitants citizens of Elysium. In order to put this revised protocol into effect, he now needs to get to Elysium, hack the central computer, and reboot the system. Following a generic action-adventure scenario in which Frey, Max, and Spider's gang make their way to Elysium and battle their way to the space station's central information hub, the insurgents successfully hack and reboot the system. Max does not survive the data transfer, but Frey and Spider live to see the institution of a new world order. The movie ends with law-enforcement droids on Elysium refusing to arrest the rebels, who are now Elysian citizens, while the central government computer calculates the number of citizens in need of medical attention on Earth and starts dispatching medical ships to the planet. The closing images show hoards of slum dwellers rushing to board the rescue crafts that will take them to the floating Crystal Palace.

This utopian resolution that *Elysium* proposes to the social contradictions depicted in the film might appear simplistic, but it in fact follows the general logic of the proposition put forth by Vladimir Lenin in "Can the Bolsheviks Retain State Power?" (1917), written on the eve of the October Revolution. Referring specifically to the big banks—a "'state apparatus' which we *need* to bring about socialism, and which we *take ready-made* from capitalism"—Lenin argues that "our task here is merely to *lop off* what *capitalistically mutilates* this excellent apparatus, to make it *even bigger*, even more democratic, even more comprehensive."[37] Assuring his comrades that they can "lay hold of" this apparatus "at one stroke, by a single decree," Lenin proposes not to do away with the big banks but, on the contrary, to seize control of them and put them to work for the benefit of the many instead of the profit of the few. When Max and his band of unlikely Bolsheviks storm the Crystal Palace and hack into the system, reconfiguring society with a keystroke, they perform a comparable operation. Expropriating the expropriators and bursting asunder society's capitalist integument, these ragtag revolutionaries in effect "*lop off* what *capitalistically mutilates*" Elysium's extraordinary health

148

care system, making it work for the benefit of all instead of the tiny minority of the super-rich and the inordinately privileged.

Pariahs of the World, Unite!

We will see below that *Snowpiercer* proposes a very different solution to a substantially similar problem. Before leaving *Elysium*, I want to add a few closing words about the motley conglomeration of have-nots depicted in the film. As we have seen, this heterogeneous group is composed in part of workers currently employed, however precariously, in sectors as different as health care and arms manufacturing. Juxtaposed to these wage laborers is the anonymous mass of the unemployed. The film does not provide much detail about members of the latter group, but we can infer that some of them (such as the beer drinkers that mock Max for going to work) have essentially dropped out of the labor market, while others (such as those to whom the Armadyne foreman indirectly alludes) form an industrial reserve army of currently unemployed but potentially employable prospective workers. In the brilliant penultimate subchapter of *Valences of the Dialectic*, Fredric Jameson subsumes these three groups, to which he adds the category of "the *formerly employed*: that is to say, the working populations once active in vital industries which have now ceased to function," under the general rubric of *those opposed to the system*: "As an historical matter," Jameson writes in reference to the pauperized of society (a classification that would prospectively include the formerly employed along with the temporarily unemployed and the structurally unemployable), "the latter are in fact gradually absorbed into those mass disturbances which develop into political revolutions, whose structure consists in a tendential yet absolute dichotomization of society into two great classes: those for and those against."[38] In sum, Jameson argues, it is not only the traditional working class that foments revolutions. Subalterns of various stripes join forces in revolutionary upheavals against the

149

ruling class.

In his sympathetic critique of this argument, Slavoj Žižek suggests substituting the category of the *illegally employed* for that of the *formerly employed*.[39] The inclusion of this new group is important given the expansion of the so-called "informal economy" in recent decades. According to Davis, this sector "currently employs 57 percent of the workforce and supplies four out of five new 'jobs'" in Latin America. Indeed, he adds parenthetically, "the *only* jobs created in Mexico between 2000 and 2004 were in the informal sector."[40] Given that Blomkamp bases his future Los Angeles on the mega-slums east of present-day Mexico City, these statistics make the inclusion of Spider's character all the more relevant. Granted, Spider is not an illegal employee but, rather, an illegal employer running an illicit business in a forbidden trade. However, these aspects of Spider's professional life serve to emphasize the illegality of his work. Although he may not be emblematic of the booming informal sector, the type of work he does is very much a part of it.

When Spider and his band of human smugglers and gunrunners join forces with Max and Frey, they enable us to envision a coalition of society's pariahs fighting in common cause against the wealthy elite. This is not traditional class conflict, but it is class conflict nonetheless. What the film beckons us to envisage is a class war waged not by the working class alone, but by an expanded supra-class that would include the deviant, the discarded, and the destitute along with the exploited. Given the changes that global capitalism has undergone over the past 4 decades and the prospect of current trends to continue into the future, it is precisely such a re-conception of the forces of resistance that we need to imagine if we do not want to live in a world like the one depicted in *Elysium*.

A Capitalist Disaster

Released the same year as *Elysium*, Bong Joon-ho's *Snowpiercer* presents an even starker, more pared-down, and more explicitly allegorical transposition of anti-capitalist sentiment into sounds and moving images. As in Blomkamp's science-fiction future, the world in Bong's sci-fi dystopia is sharply divided along class lines. Both movies represent this class division by means of a rigorously segregated social space that gives each film its title, and both depict the revolt of the underclass against a powerful elite. However, the rebels in *Snowpiercer* are even lower on the social scale than their counterparts in *Elysium*, and the resolution that Bong offers to the class conflict is all the more radical. I propose here to sketch in broad strokes the narrative trajectory of Bong's anti-capitalist allegory, to contemplate the all-out class war it depicts, and to ponder the social implications of the anti-utopian resolution it proposes.

Snowpiercer initially introduces its anti-capitalist stance subtly, in the narrative exposition that sets up the story at the beginning of the film, when over a black screen we hear fragmented news reports of how on July 1, 2014 (11 months to the day after the movie opened in South Korea), 79 countries dispersed a chemical called CW-7 into the upper layers of the Earth's atmosphere in an attempt to reverse global warming. A single ground-level shot of jet airplanes streaming across the blue sky, leaving wide trails in their wake, concludes this brief introduction. The scene then cuts back to black, the film title appears on the screen, and a somber cartoon-like image of a frozen landscape fades into view. We soon learn that the artificial cooling agent worked better than expected, turning the Earth into a frozen wasteland, and that the precious few survivors of the Great Freeze boarded the Snowpiercer, a miles-long locomotive that has been ceaselessly circling the planet ever since. Set on New Year's Eve of 2031, the remainder of Bong's post-apocalyptic thriller takes place almost entirely within the confines of this high-speed train. All we see of the outside world are a snow-covered landscape, abandoned cities, and frozen remnants of a dead civilization.

Although this introductory narrative exposition does not explicitly blame the environmental disaster on capitalism, it calls the culprit to mind without naming it. As Naomi Klein shows in *This Changes Everything: Capitalism vs. the Climate* (2014), capitalist production and global warming have become two facets of the same process. At this point in time, Klein argues, one cannot counteract the latter without combating the former. "What the climate needs to avoid collapse is a contraction of humanity's use of resources," she writes. "What our economic model demands to avoid collapse is unfettered expansion."[41] The opening minutes of *Snowpiercer* present and roundly critique attempts, not unlike ones currently under investigation in scientific circles, to overcome this contradiction. As Klein reports, geo-engineers have been developing technological fixes that might enable humanity to continue spewing greenhouse gases into the atmosphere without suffering the environmental consequences. The cooling method that scientists consider the "most plausible and promising," Klein recounts, is Solar Radiation Management. This method, the very one used in the opening sequence of *Snowpiercer*, involves "injecting particles into the atmosphere in order to reflect more sunlight back to space, thereby reducing the amount of heat that reaches the earth."[42] As science historian James Fleming warns, such a scheme is "untested and untestable, and dangerous beyond belief."[43] The only way to know whether it might work would be to use our existing planet in an irreversible global experiment. "What could possibly go wrong?" Klein rhetorically asks, tongue very much in cheek. *Snowpiercer*'s prologue offers a pointed response to that question.

The Capitalist Machine

In sum, *Snowpiercer*'s introductory narrative exposition provides a plausible explanation for the imaginary future state of the biosphere and implicitly implicates capitalism in the environmental catastrophe it envisions. The movie's central metaphor for the dynamics of capitalism takes the opposite approach. It is neither subtle nor realistic. The cartoonish aesthetic adopted for the train sequences, which sharply contrast with the naturalistic look of the low-angle shot of the overhead jets in the narrative prologue, not only pays homage to the movie's source material in Jacques Lob and Jean-Marc Rochette's 1982 graphic novel, *Le Transperceneige*. It also signals the purely allegorical dimensions of the world depicted on the screen. Before getting into the film's narrative development, let us briefly examine the peculiar properties of the train that gives the movie its title, and the ways that this high-speed locomotive transcodes diverse facets of global capitalism into a single composite image.

Each of the Snowpiercer's compartments serves a specific function. The first-class sections toward the front of the train cater to the needs of the leisure class. There is a magnificent aquarium populated with exotic fish, an abutting dining car where sushi is served, a rail car housing a well maintained terrarium, a high-class café car, a coach that serves as a schoolhouse where children are indoctrinated to the worldview (or "train-view") of the ruling class, and a drug den where self-indulgent members of the bourgeoisie can cater to their addiction to Kronole, a narcotic made from the engine's toxic waste. Toward the rear of the train are "the hallowed water supply section" and the room where millipedes are ground into the greasy, gelatinous "protein blocks" that the underclass are fed. At the very back of the train the underprivileged live in squalor, while at the opposite end "the sacred engine" keeps the machine running. There appears to be no communication between the back and the front of the train other than the periodic visits that the huddled masses receive from armed guards and cryptic notes that mysteriously appear in the starving multitude's protein blocks. The train's spatial configuration presents in this way a graphic and decidedly unsubtle hierarchized class structure, which literally compartmentalizes the different social strata in fixed positions.

This social division is not really a split between capital and labor. In contrast to the film world of *Elysium*, for example, there is neither a working class nor a bona fide capitalist class in Bong's science-fiction future. Indeed, there is no wage labor at all in *Snowpiercer*, where all that remains of the human race is an idle leisure class that lives in comfort and security at the front of the locomotive, a mass of supernumerary beings quarantined like animals at the back of the train, and an array of soldiers and officers whose job it is to maintain the Snowpiercer's strictly regimented order. Allegorically, however, this post-capitalist future very much refracts our advanced capitalist present. Its central image of a train that continually circles the planet at a frenetic pace functions as a loud and clunky metaphor for global capital itself. Simultaneously codifying a rigid class system and allegorizing the capitalist machine as such, the Snowpiercer is a composite visual metaphor that condenses the capitalist means of production, the circulation of global capital, and a stratified class society into a single image.

The film provides no explanation for why this massive locomotive must continually circumnavigate the planet. It presents the necessity of the train's perpetual movement as an unelaborated and unexplained fact. In the fictional film world, that is just the way it is. Rather than faulting the film for failing to elucidate the train's compulsory nonstop circuit, I take this lack of explication to be one of the movie's strengths. The unquestioned belief, shared by everyone aboard the Snowpiercer, that the train must perpetually tour the planet without stopping forms the unstated *doxa* of Bong's near-future dystopia. It functions, in the film, much like French Marxist Louis Althusser's influential theory that ideology is first and foremost the unquestioned "obviousness" of the way things are, "Yes, that's how it is, that's really true!" being the quintessential ideological supposition.[44]

By refraining from offering even a rudimentary explanation for the perpetual-motion machine in *Snowpiercer*, Bong wordlessly situates the universally held belief that the engine must keep running in the realm of ideology.

Given the movie's unsubtle evocations of capitalist globalization in the allegorical mode, the content of this ideological supposition calls to mind the Thatcher doctrine that "there is no alternative" to global capitalism. This neoliberal slogan, which gives Mark Fisher's *Capitalist Realism: Is There No Alternative?* (2009) its subtitle, dismisses alternatives to global capitalism not by critiquing or refuting them, but by relegating them to the domain of the unthinkable. The idea that there was no alternative to the unfettered expansion of global capital was hotly contested in the 1980s, when Margaret Thatcher proposed it. Keynesian economics, which tempered the excesses of capitalism, still held sway in much of the West. When US President Ronald Reagan fired striking air traffic controllers in 1981 and Prime Minister Thatcher broke the back of the miners' union in 1985, they ushered in a new era of industrial-labor relations in the West. With the fall of the Berlin Wall a few years later, the huge global counter-weight to laissez-faire economics finally vanished. With it, the last obstacle to capitalist globalization disappeared. Consequently, Fisher remarks, for most people born in Europe and North America after the 1980s, "the lack of alternatives to capitalism is no longer even an issue. Capitalism seamlessly occupies the horizons of the thinkable."[45] Likewise, for the "train babies" born after 2014, who know nothing but life aboard the Snowpiercer, the idea of existence beyond the confines of the train is inconceivable.

The limitless expanse of frozen wasteland glimpsed outside the train's windows serves a complementary function. It crystallizes, for film viewers and passengers alike, the palpable lack of an alternative to life on the train. It thereby serves, within the film's diegesis, an ideological function not unlike the one that the specter of totalitarian communism has historically played in the non-filmic First World. *See where your utopian dreams of universal equality lead?* supporters of the capitalist status quo can ask, pointing to the horrors of "really existing socialism." *Straight to the Gulag and the killing fields!* In a similar way, the desolate landscape viewed through the train's windows puts a damper on whatever aspirations the train dwellers might have for a different world. As imperfect and inequitable as life on the Snowpiercer may be, it is preferable to the vast Siberia on the other side of the glass panes.

Derailing Capitalism

Our first glimpse inside the Snowpiercer conveys why train dwellers might aspire to a world different from the one in which they live. Following the expository prologue and a couple of exterior shots of the locomotive rattling past a parking lot full of frozen cars, the movie begins with the arrival of armed guards at the back of the train. Rows of downtrodden people dressed in rags and covered with filth line up for a head-count. These abject beings sit subserviently as their rows are called. Only one man remains standing when the guards count his row, signaling the beginning of the rebellion that constitutes the movie's plot.

The first half-hour of this 126-minute film is dominated by debates among members of the tail section over the timing and the leadership of the uprising. The crucial question of timing is raised from the first exchange between Curtis (Chris Evans), the man who refuses to sit down when the guards call his row, and Edgar (Jamie Bell), his sidekick. Initially it is Edgar that urges his companion to sit down; later Curtis orders Edgar to temper his outbursts, informing his adjunct that "now isn't the time" to revolt. Similar discussions take place between Curtis and Tanya (Octavia Spenser), who becomes one of the most committed revolutionaries on the train after the authorities abduct her son, and Gilliam (John Hurt), a respected elder of the tail section.

Echoing perennial debates among militant revolutionaries, these exchanges function as shorthand evocations of polemics that rage between different revolutionary factions in times of social unrest. In his gloss of the events leading up to the October Revolution of 1917, for example, Slavoj Žižek recounts how "the Menshevik stance was that of obedience to the logic of the 'objective stages of development,'" whereas "the Leninist stance was to take a leap, throwing oneself into the paradox of the situation, seizing the opportunity and intervening, even if the situation was 'premature,' with a wager that this very 'premature' intervention would radically change the 'objective' relationship of forces."[46] In *History and Class Consciousness* (1923), the Hungarian Marxist Georg Lukács proposes a similar interpretation of the debate between Rosa Luxemburg and Eduard Bernstein at the turn of the twentieth century. "As early as her first polemic with Bernstein," Lukács writes, Luxemburg "argued that the necessary 'premature' seizure of power by the proletariat was inevitable. She unmasked the resulting opportunist fear and lack of faith in revolution as 'political nonsense which starts from the assumption that society progresses mechanically.'"[47] Žižek, in turn, reads Lukács' own concept of the *Augenblick*— "the moment when, briefly, there is an opening for an act to intervene in a situation" — in a similar vein. "The crux of Lukács' argumentation is to reject the reduction of the act to its 'historical circumstances,'" Žižek writes; for Lukács, "there are no neutral 'objective conditions.'"[48]

The *Augenblick* in *Snowpiercer* comes when Curtis realizes that the guards have no bullets or else they would have already shot at the unruly mob at the back of the train. Testing this theory, Curtis marches directly to an armed guard, puts the gun barrel to his own forehead, and squeezes the trigger. At the sound of the click, his comrades leap into action, overpowering the guard detail and making their way to the quarantine section. There they spring the imprisoned Namgoong ("Nam") Minsoo

(Kang-ho Song), a security expert and Kronole addict, and his daughter, Yona (Ko Asung), whom they bribe into unlocking the gates separating the various train sections in exchange for drugs: "Every door you open," Curtis explains, "you get one lump of Kronole." The next hour of the film shows the revolutionary brigade fighting its way past successive waves of guards, soldiers, and assassins, each group more formidable than the last, until the insurgents finally reach the engine room. The rebels' numbers have diminished at this point to single digits, the vast majority of the combatants having died in battle along the way. The film then ends with a series of interrelated plot twists.

The first twist occurs when Curtis is invited into the engine room, where the mythical Wilford (Ed Harris), builder of the train and driver of the engine, divulges that he and Gilliam, his contact in the tail section, instigated the rebellion in the aim of thinning out the train's population. Explaining that the train is a closed ecosystem where air, water, food supply, and population must be kept in balance, Wilford confesses that the only way to achieve the proper balance is periodically to implement "more radical solutions": "We don't have time for true natural selection," the trainmaster explains. "We would all be hideously overcrowded and starved waiting for that. The next best solution is to have individual units kill off other individual units." Evoking past rebellions as well as the current one that brought Curtis to the head of the train, Wilford recounts how he and Gilliam worked in cooperation in order to determine when such drastic measures should be taken. The cryptic messages that had been appearing in the lumpens' protein blocks, with words like "Nam" (giving the name of the imprisoned security specialist that the insurgents should spring in order to unlock the gates) and "water" (indicating the rail car that the rebels must capture if they want to control the train), were not written by an anonymous informant from the front section but, on the contrary, in collusion with a collaborator embedded in the tail section.

Having revealed the Curtis Rebellion to be a ruse of history, in which the rebels' assault on the engine inadvertently contributed to the smooth functioning of the machine, Wilford then admits that in this particular case, the rebels were more successful than anticipated. No previous group had ever made it all the way to the front, Curtis now being the only person in train history to have walked the entire length of the locomotive. He then writes a final note and hands it to the rebel leader: "train," indicating the aging engine driver's wish for Curtis to take over his position at the head of the Snowpiercer.

This last message recalls the second discussion topic debated during the first half-hour of the film. Everyone in the tail section agrees that the revolution needs a leader. Curtis thinks it should be Gilliam, the oldest, most experienced, and most respected member of the tail section, while everyone else, the duplicitous Gilliam included, thinks it should be Curtis. A strong argument in favor of Curtis' leadership is his commitment to changing the social configuration of the train and not simply replacing one dominant class with another. In response to Edgar's castigation of the "bastards at the front of the train [that] think they own us, eating their steak dinner and listening to string quartets and that," for instance, Curtis declares: "We'll be different when we get there."

The bitter irony here is that Curtis accepts Wilford's offer to run the train when he finally confronts the engine driver at the end of the film. Curtis' refusal to give Yona the match she needs to detonate the explosives that she and Nam, the only other surviving insurgents at this point, have attached to an outside door signals his change of alliance. Rather than handing her the matchbook, he extends his hand to stop her in her tracks and then, hand still extended toward her, silently removes himself from her. A shot of Curtis and Wilford standing side-by-side, framed by the churning cylindrical engine chamber while looking down at Yona, depicts the ascension of the new trainmaster.

Yona then strikes upon the idea that will change Curtis' mind. Without speaking, she pries open a trapdoor to the gearbox below the engine-room floor. Integrated into the gears is Timmy (Marcanthonee Reis), the son of the martyred Tanya, who now functions as an organic replacement for an extinct machine part. After a moment's hesitation, Curtis inserts his arm into the churning gears, temporarily stopping the engine at the cost of a limb, while throwing Yona the matches with his free hand.

Yona then lights the fuse, blowing open the side door to the outside world and triggering an avalanche that derails the Snowpiercer. This cataclysmic finale kills everyone aboard the train except Yona and Timmy, whom Nam and Curtis shield with their bodies, forming a protective cocoon around the young woman and the little boy. The movie's last shots show these two survivors emerging from the wreckage and stepping out into the snowy wilderness. Dressed in fur coats and boots, the two train babies silently take stock of their new situation. Scanning the snow-covered mountains that surround them, they spy a polar bear on the horizon, giving the lie to the prevailing *doxa* that life outside the train is impossible.

The Revolt of the Lumpenproletariat

One of the salient aspects of this politically potent anti-capitalist allegory is the non-workers cast in the role of revolutionaries. Both visually and narratively, the grime- and filth-covered subalterns who take up arms in *Snowpiercer* evoke the "lumpenproletariat" rather than the proletarian vanguard that Marx sees leading the revolution. According to Marx, this abject subclass, which he occasionally recognizes as a social class unto itself, historically sides with counter-revolutionary forces. In his book on the reactionary 1851 coup d'état of Louis-Napoléon Bonaparte, for example, Marx asserts that "this Bonaparte, who constitutes himself *chief of the lumpenproletariat*, [...] recognizes in this scum, offal, refuse of all classes the only class upon which he can base himself unconditionally."[49] In the eyes of Marx's anarchist rival Mikhail Bakunin, by contrast, this non-class class constitutes one of the great hopes for the social revolution. "That great rabble of the people (underdogs, 'dregs of society') ordinarily designated by Marx and Engels in the picturesque and contemptuous phrase *lumpenproletariat*," Bakunin writes, "carries in its inner being and its aspirations, in all the necessities and miseries of its collective life, all the seeds of the socialism of the future."[50] In short, as Peter Marshall concludes in his analysis of the Marx-Bakunin polemic in his comprehensive history of anarchism, "Just as Marx idealized the proletariat, so Bakunin romanticized the lumpenproletariat."[51]

The reason that Bakunin favored the rabble at the bottom of the social scale over Marx's working-class heroes is thought provoking in the current era of joblessness and job insecurity. Whereas the scientific socialist (Marx) argued that the urban proletariat's unique position in the capitalist mode of production made it the "universal" and only truly revolutionary class, the rabble-rousing anarchist held that, on the contrary, the workers' integration into the mode of production compromised their resolve. In Saul Newman's words, "Bakunin believed that the small elite of 'class-conscious' proletarians constituting the upper echelons of the working class, lived in a relatively comfortable and semi-bourgeois fashion, and had been, in fact, co-opted into the bourgeoisie."[52] Although the supposition here that employees with steady jobs are complicit with the bourgeoisie does not necessarily stand to reason, there is something to the argument that those with the least to lose have the most to gain. If, as Marx and Engels assert at the end of *The Communist Manifesto*, "the proletarians have nothing to lose but their chains," this statement is doubly true of the sub-proletarians that do not even have jobs to lose.[53]

Many of the films examined in this book include some image of the lumpens in their conception of the forces of resistance. With the ongoing redundancy of social labor and the concomitant growth of the ranks of the "precariat," the unemployed, and the unemployable, the necessity of incorporating labor-market dropouts and those with no prospect of employment into the anti-capitalist struggle becomes increasingly urgent. Social theorists and political economists who cleave too closely to the letter of Marx's text overlook the revolutionary potential of these groups at their peril. Chris Harman, for example, an erudite Marxist and an important voice on the anti-capitalist left, chastises his colleagues who "overemphasise how precarious jobs are": "Those voices on the left who exaggerate [job] insecurity can add to [the] demoralisation [of workers], rather than countering it with a recognition of the counter-factors that provide workers with continued strength if they have the confidence to deploy it."[54] As sympathetic as one may be to the tenor of this argument, its obverse is the idea that we need not concern ourselves with one of the most pernicious aspects of capitalism. In his effort to empower the traditional labor movement at all costs, Harman inadvertently fosters a quietism of a different sort while simultaneously relegating to the margins of history those that the system has thrown out of work.

Marx himself eventually revised his position on the lumpenproletariat. Whereas his early works show nothing but disdain for the "social scum" that he and Engels derisively characterize as the "passive decaying matter of the lowest layers of the old society,"[55] his crucial inclusion, in volume 1 of *Capital*, of the lumpens in the "relative surplus population" that capitalism creates as a byproduct of its development implicitly recognizes the revolutionary potential of this downtrodden group. Alongside the "floating" and "latent" relative surplus populations, which form capital's industrial reserve army, Marx places the "stagnant" segments of the population that have been cast into permanent pauperism. The latter group includes "vagabonds, criminals, prostitutes, in short the actual lumpenproletariat."[56]

What *Snowpiercer* has us envision is a world in which the working class lauded by Marx is extinct and all that remains of the once heroic proletariat is a base and dejected lumpenproletariat. Bong's vision of a world without a working class is hyperbolic, but it is the asymptotic horizon to which Marx's writings on technology lead. Although Marx does not to my knowledge contemplate the prospect of a world completely devoid of social labor, such a world is not entirely inconceivable. There will undoubtedly always be a need for some human oversight and intervention, but the idea of a world, such as the one depicted in *Snowpiercer*, where a few magnates at the top oversee general operations while a few peons at the bottom fix technical glitches is not beyond the realm of possibility. All we need to do is imagine current trends continuing unabated into the future to form a picture of what a world of that sort might look like. It is precisely such an image that *Snowpiercer* puts before our eyes.

Snowpiercer thereby conjures in its own way the two Marxian theories of the end of capitalism evoked above in our discussion of *Elysium*: one in which the system goes out with a bang, the other where it ends with a whimper. The latter of these scenarios does not take the form of falling profits in Bong's sci-fi future. Rather, it presents itself as a different consequence of the increased ratio of constant to variable capital, namely the eclipse of social labor itself. Like in Blomkamp's anti-capitalist allegory, it is the narrative of class struggle, not the change in the composition of capital, that drives *Snowpiercer*'s plot. And again like *Elysium*, *Snowpiercer* concludes with a violent "negation of the negation" that rings the death knell of capitalism. However, the forms that these two negations of the negation take in the two films differ radically. In conclusion, let us briefly examine these contrasting scenarios.

"There are," Fredric Jameson writes in *Valences of the Dialectic*, "two forms the negation of the negation can take": "On the one hand, the negation of capitalism no longer leads back to the Utopian but simply destroys the preexisting form itself; on the other, it constitutes a progression within the system itself toward greater and greater complexity and 'modernity.'"[57] This characterization of the contrasting forms that the negation of the negation can take seems tailor-made for the different narrative conclusions to *Elysium* and *Snowpiercer*. Whereas *Elysium* culminates with a negation of the negation on the order of the second version described here by Jameson, *Snowpiercer* presents a demolition of the apparatus along the lines of the first version. In one case, the insurgents appropriate the state's excellent apparatus and make it even bigger, more complex, more comprehensive, and more democratic; in the other, they send the entire machine, from engine to caboose, into a ravine. In contrast to their revolutionary counterparts in *Elysium*, who reconfigure the existing apparatus for the benefit of the many, the anarchists of *Snowpiercer* reduce it to rubble.

Here again the Marx-Bakunin polemic is instructive. Although Marx does not rule out the possibility of armed struggle, the social revolution that he envisages need not take the form of violent confrontations in the streets. By virtue of their indispensable position in the mode of production, proletarians can parlay their collective power on the factory floor into a political power that they wield directly. To the extent that it violates the existing capitalist-parliamentary system, this appropriation of the state apparatus is violent, but it does not necessarily entail bloody battles on the barricades. Following a transitional phase that Marx famously calls "the dictatorship of the proletariat," the state can then "wither away." Bakunin, by contrast, calls for the violent destruction of the state. "If there is a State," he argues, "there must be domination of one class by another and, as a result, slavery; the State without slavery is unthinkable—and this is why we are enemies of the State."[58] Whence his calls for a "complete annihilation" of the state, which can only occur by "blood and fire," a "furious avalanche, devouring, destroying everything."[59] For better or worse, it is the latter resolution to the class conflict that *Snowpiercer* ultimately proposes. With the tendential redundancy of social labor and the ongoing conversion of the working class into a formless mass of lumpens, it is, unfortunately, a vision that has become all too timely. As the system disposes of the once indispensable working class, the ability of this group, whose power diminishes with its numbers, to wield real political power shrinks proportionally. At this point a mass insurrection by the lumpenproletariat is more plausible than a dictatorship of the proletariat.

In its final plot twist, the film then leads us from despair to an ambiguous but unequivocal hope. Having convinced us for 2 hours that the barren and desolate snow-covered landscape does not support organic life, the movie ends with an image of life outside the train. To the extent that the Snowpiercer represents global capitalism, which is a great extent indeed, the powerful and evocative closing shots of the polar bear on the horizon function allegorically as a visual refutation of the prevailing wisdom that there is no alternative to the unimpeded progress of the capitalist machine. Existence in the snowy wilderness will undoubtedly be difficult. Yona and Timmy might not survive, but the bear's presence provides proof positive that life exists outside the train. Offering an affirmative response to the question that Fisher asks in the subtitle of his book, *there is an alternative* to the infernal machine's inexorable progress at any cost. Life beyond capitalism exists.

Endnotes

Introduction

1. Frantz Fanon, *The Wretched of the Earth*, trans. Richard Philcox (New York: Grove Press, 2004), 6.

2. Karl Marx and Friedrich Engels, *The Communist Manifesto* (Oxford: Oxford University Press, 1998), 14.

3. Siegfried Kracauer, *The Mass Ornament: Weimar Essays*, ed. and trans. Thomas Y. Levin (Cambridge, MA: Harvard University Press, 1995), 75.

4. Siegfried Kracauer, *From Caligari to Hitler: A Psychological History of the German Film*, revised and expanded ed. (Princeton: Princeton University Press, 2004), 6.

5. Ibid.

6. Ibid., 7.

7. Cited in Leonardo Quaresima, introduction to *From Caligari to Hitler: A Psychological History of the German Film*, by Siegfried Kracauer, revised and expanded ed. (Princeton: Princeton University Press, 2004), xxviii.

8. See Kracauer, *From Caligari to Hitler*, 5–6.

9. See Fredric Jameson, "Cognitive Mapping," in *Marxism and the Interpretation of Culture*, ed. Cary Nelson and Lawrence Grossberg (Champaign: University of Illinois Press, 1988), 347–60; Jameson, *Postmodernism, or, The Cultural Logic of Late Capitalism* (Durham: Duke University Press, 1991), 45–54 and 399–418.

10. Reading Robert Paxton's *Anatomy of Fascism* (New York: Vintage, 2004) after the 2016 election of Donald Trump is illuminating in this regard.

Chapter 1 The End of the World of the End: *Melancholia*

1. Steven Shaviro, *"Melancholia*, or, the Romantic Anti-Sublime," *Sequence* 1, no. 1 (2012), http://reframe.sussex.

ac.uk/sequence1/1-1-melancholia-or-the-romantic-anti-sublime/.

2. Fredric Jameson, *The Political Unconscious: Narrative as a Socially Symbolic Act* (Ithaca: Cornell University Press, 1981), 17, 20.

3. Manohla Dargis, "This is How the End Begins," *New York Times*, December 30, 2011, http://www.nytimes.com/2012/01/01/movies/awardsseason/manohla-dargis-looks-at-the-overture-to-melancholia.html?_r=1.

4. The film industry's obsession with producing audience-pleasing endings is perhaps nowhere more evident than in the questionnaires circulated by movie studios at advance film screenings. Roughly half of these questionnaires, at least in the case of the advance screening I attended, are dedicated to checking whether the sample audience finds the ending satisfying.

5. For a compelling alternate reading of this sequence, see Marta Figlerowicz, "Comedy of Abandon: Lars von Trier's *Melancholia*," *Film Quarterly* 65, no. 4 (2012): 23. My appreciation of von Trier's aesthetic owes a debt to Figlerowicz's insightful article.

6. Shaviro, "Romantic Anti-Sublime."

7. For a reading of the "loser wins" *topos* in Sartre's work, see Philip Knee, *Qui perd gagne: essai sur Sartre* (Laval: Presses Universitaires de Laval, 1993).

8. Shaviro, "Romantic Anti-Sublime."

9. Kojève is an intriguing figure whose legacy bifurcated along continental lines. On the one hand, Kojève's well-attended Paris lectures influenced a generation of radical French thinkers including the likes of Georges Bataille, Jacques Lacan, and Jean-Paul Sartre. In the United States, on the other hand, following a trajectory that led from Leo Strauss to Allan Bloom, and from Bloom to Fukuyama, his legacy became intertwined with the rise of the neoconservative

movement.

10. Alexandre Kojève, *Introduction to the Reading of Hegel: Lectures on the Phenomenology of Spirit*, assembled by Raymond Queneau, ed. Alan Bloom, trans. James H. Nichols, Jr. (Ithaca: Cornell University Press, 1980), 44.

11. Francis Fukuyama, *The End of History and the Last Man* (New York: Free Press, 2006), xii.

12. Ibid.

13. Ibid., 205.

14. Ibid., 66.

15. Ibid., xiii.

16. Ibid., xiii–xiv.

17. Jacques Derrida, *Specters of Marx*, trans. Peggy Kamuf (New York: Routledge, 1994), 78.

18. Fukuyama, *End of History*, xiv.

19. Slavoj Žižek, *In Defense of Lost Causes* (London: Verso, 2008), 421.

20. Slavoj Žižek, "Class Struggle or Postmodernism? Yes, please!" in Judith Butler, Ernesto Laclau, and Slavoj Žižek, *Contingency, Hegemony, Universality* (London: Verso, 2000), 95.

21. Mark Fisher, *Capitalist Realism: Is There No Alternative?* (Winchester, UK: Zero Books, 2009), 6.

22. Ibid., 2.

23. Ibid., 8.

24. Ibid., 8–9.

25. Ibid., 6.

26. See Giorgio Agamben, *Homo Sacer: Sovereign Power and Bare Life*, trans. Daniel Heller-Roazen (Stanford: Stanford University Press, 1998), 63–67; Judith Butler, "Critique, Coercion, and Sacred Life in Benjamin's 'Critique of Violence,'" in *Political Theologies: Public Religions in a Post-Secular World*, eds. Hent de Vries and Lawrence E. Sullivan (Bronx, NY: Fordham University Press, 2006), 201–19; Simon

Critchley, *The Faith of the Faithless: Experiments in Political Theology* (London: Verso, 2012), 207–45; Jacques Derrida, "Force of Law: The 'Mystical Foundation of Authority,'" in *Acts of Religion*, ed. Gil Anidjar (New York: Routledge, 2002), 228–98; Slavoj Žižek, *Violence: Six Sideways Reflections* (New York: Picador, 2009), 196–205.

27. Žižek, *Violence*, 196–97.
28. Ibid., 9.
29. Ibid., 196; Slavoj Žižek, "Robespierre, or the Divine Violence of Terror," in *Žižek Presents Robespierre: Virtue and Terror*, ed. Jean Ducange (London: Verso, 2007), x–xi.
30. Žižek, *Violence*, 199–200.
31. Walter Benjamin, *Selected Writings*, vol. 1, ed. Marcus Bullock and Michael W. Jennings (Cambridge, MA: Harvard University Press, 2004), 250.
32. Ibid.
33. Critchley, *Faith of the Faithless*, 216.
34. Micah White, *The End of Protest: A New Playbook for Revolution* (Toronto: Knopf Canada, 2016), 9.
35. Ibid., 10.
36. Kurt Andersen, "Person of the Year 2011: The Protestor," *Time*, December 14, 2011, http://content.time.com/time/specials/packages/article/0,28804,2101745_2102132,00.html.
37. Alain Badiou, *The Rebirth of History: Times of Riots and Uprisings*, trans. Gregory Elliott (London: Verso, 2012), 5.
38. Slavoj Žižek, *The Year of Dreaming Dangerously* (London: Verso, 2012), 77.
39. Ibid.
40. Ibid., 53.
41. Ibid., 60.
42. Benjamin, *Selected Writings*, 245.
43. Žižek, *Year of Dreaming Dangerously*, 54.
44. Ibid., 53.
45. White, *End of Protest*, 34.

46. Ibid., 35.

47. Ibid., 26.

48. "Oxfam Says Wealth of Richest 1% Equal to Other 99%," *BBC*, January 18, 2016, http://www.bbc.com/news/business-35339475.

49. Ibid.

50. White, *End of Protest*, 26.

51. Ibid., 28.

52. Ibid., 43.

53. Ibid., 160.

54. Ibid., 46–47.

55. Critchley, *Faith of the Faithless*, 24.

56. Ibid., 25.

57. Ibid., 220.

58. Ibid., 217. I am cherry-picking passages from Critchley's book that work within the context of my argument here. For a more nuanced appreciation of Critchley's overall contribution in *Faith of the Faithless*, see Milo Sweedler, "The Poison and the Cure—Experiments in Political Theology: Critchley's *The Faith of the Faithless*." *Theory & Event* 15, no. 3 (2012), http://muse.jhu.edu/journals/theory_and_event/v015/15.3.sweedler.html.

59. Fredric Jameson, "Future City," *New Left Review* 21 (May–June 2003), 76.

60. Fredric Jameson, *The Seeds of Time* (New York: Columbia University Press, 1994), xii. Matthew Beaumont traces the original association of the end of capitalism and the end of the world to an essay by H. Bruce Franklin on J.G. Ballard, which concludes with the question: "What could Ballard create if he were able to envision the end of capitalism as not the end, but the beginning, of a human world?" As Beaumont remarks, Jameson silently turns Franklin's conclusion on its head. See Matthew Beaumont, "Imagining the End Times: Ideology, the Contemporary Disaster Movie, *Contagion*,"

in *Žižek and Media Studies: A Reader* (New York: Palgrave Macmillan, 2014), ed. Matthew Flisfeder and Louis-Paul Willis, 88.

61. See Beaumont, "Imagining the End Times," 79.
62. Fisher, *Capitalist Realism*, 2.
63. Shaviro, "Romantic Anti-Sublime."

Chapter 2 The Demise of Finance Capital: *Cosmopolis*

1. On the MacGuffin—Alfred Hitchcock's term for the unexplained and irrelevant plot element that sets the narrative in motion—see François Truffaut, *Hitchcock*, revised ed. (New York: Simon & Schuster, 1984), 137–39, 145, 167–68.
2. See "List of People Who Have Been Pied," *Wikipedia*, https://en.wikipedia.org/wiki/List_of_people_who_have_been_pied.
3. Don DeLillo, *Cosmopolis* (New York: Scribner, 2003), 209.
4. David Cronenberg, "Audio commentary." *Cosmopolis*, directed by David Cronenberg (Toronto: Entertainment One, 2013).
5. Kirk Boyle, "Three Ways of Looking at a Neoliberalist: Mobile Global Traffic in *Cosmopolis* and *Nightcrawler*," *Quarterly Review of Film and Video* 34, no. 6 (2017): 536.
6. Caetlin Benson-Allott, "The Minor Cronenberg," *New Review of Film and Television Studies* 15, no. 2 (2017): 158.
7. Boyle, "Three Ways," 541.
8. Ibid.
9. See for example Karl Marx, *A Contribution to the Critique of Political Economy*, trans. N.I. Stone (New York: International Publishers, 1970), 41; Marx, *Capital*, vol. 1, trans. Ben Fowkes (London: Penguin, 1976), 92, 254. For an illuminating reading of the first passage, see Fredric Jameson, *Representing Capital* (London: Verso, 2011), 29–31. For a compelling analysis of the other two passages, see Alberto Toscano and Jeff Kinkle,

Cartographies of the Absolute (Winchester, UK: Zero Books, 2015), 40–44.

10. Jameson, *Representing Capital,* 64.
11. Ibid., 114.
12. Ibid., 41.
13. Ibid.
14. Ibid., 114.
15. David Graeber, *Debt: The First 5,000 Years,* updated and expanded ed. (Brooklyn: Melville House, 2014), 17.
16. Amy Taubin, review of *Cosmopolis,* directed by David Cronenberg, *Artforum* 51, no. 1 (September 2012): 471.
17. Benson-Allott, "Minor Cronenberg," 159.
18. Cited in ibid.
19. Ibid.
20. Ibid.
21. Ibid.
22. Boyle, "Three Ways," 538.
23. Roger Moore, review of *Cosmopolis,* directed by David Cronenberg, *Lexington Herald Leader,* October 11, 2012, http://www.kentucky.com/entertainment/movies-news-reviews/article44381946.html.
24. Bertolt Brecht, *Brecht on Theatre,* ed. and trans. John Willett (New York: Hill and Wang, 1957), 54.
25. Ibid., 58.
26. Ibid., 91.
27. Ibid., 92–93.
28. Fredric Jameson, *Brecht and Method* (London: Verso, 1999), 50.
29. Ibid.
30. Ibid.
31. Ibid., 32.
32. Ibid., 104.
33. See Jean-Paul Sartre, *Being and Nothingness,* trans. Hazel E. Barnes (New York: Washington Square Press, 1956), 101–03.

34. Jameson, *Brecht*, 105.
35. Brecht, *Brecht on Theatre*, 140.
36. Jameson, *Brecht*, 50.
37. Ibid., 50–51.
38. Brecht, *Brecht on Theatre*, 72.
39. James Slaymaker, review of *Cosmopolis*, directed by David Cronenberg, *Film International* 12, no. 4 (December 2014): 128.
40. The inverted bell curve in Figure I.1 of Piketty's book graphs this trend in the United States with remarkable clarity. See Thomas Piketty, *Capital in the Twenty-First Century*, trans. Arthur Goldhammer (Cambridge, MA: Harvard University Press, 2014), 24. Other data presented in Piketty's book show similar trends in other countries.
41. Ibid., 265.
42. Harvey, *Brief History*, 161.
43. Ibid., 33.
44. See David Harvey, *The Enigma of Capital and the Crises of Capitalism*, with a new afterword (Oxford; Oxford University Press, 2011), 22; Piketty, *Capital in the Twenty-First Century*, 24.
45. Karl Marx, *Capital*, vol. 3, trans. David Fernbach (London: Penguin, 1981), 608.
46. Harvey, *Enigma*, 30.
47. See for example Jameson, *Postmodernism*, especially 45–54 and 399–418; Toscano and Kinkle, *Cartographies*, esp. 33–48 and 157–83.
48. Boyle, "Three Ways," 554.
49. Jameson, *Representing Capital*, 2.
50. Boyle, "Three Ways," 554.
51. David Harvey, *Seventeen Contradictions and the End of Capitalism* (Oxford: Oxford University Press, 2014), 110.
52. Slavoj Žižek, *First as Tragedy, Then as Farce* (London: Verso, 2009), 103.

53. Ibid.

54. See Karl Marx, "Economic and Philosophical Manuscripts," trans. T.B. Bottomore, in Erich Fromm, *Marx's Concept of Man* (New York: Frederick Ungar, 1961), 93–109.

55. Fromm, *Marx's Concept of Man*, 57.

56. Cited in Harvey, *Seventeen Contradictions*, 271.

57. Ibid., 271–72.

Chapter 3 The Rationality of Revolt: *Suffragette*

1. For an elaboration of the 6 years' worth of research that went into making the film, see Sarah Gavron, "The Making of the Feature Film *Suffragette*," *Women's History Review* 24, no. 6 (2015): 985–95, http://dx.doi.org/10.1080/09612025.201 5.1074007.

2. Reproductions of anti-suffragette propaganda can be found at http://historyoffeminism.com/anti-suffragette-postcards-posters-cartoons/. For a dossier of arguments pronounced in Parliament against the Votes for Women campaign, see http://www.johndclare.net/Women1_ArgumentsAgainst. htm.

3. In the feature commentary with director Sarah Gavron and screenwriter Abi Morgan included as a bonus feature on the DVD, Gavron calls attention to the irony of having been granted permission to film scenes from *Suffragette* in the very location from where women were forcibly expelled during the Votes for Women campaign. *Suffragette*, directed by Sarah Gavron (Universal City, CA: Universal, 2016), DVD.

4. Jill Liddington, *Rebel Girls: Their Fight for the Vote* (London: Virago, 2006), ix.

5. Simone de Beauvoir, *The Second Sex*, trans. Constance Borde and Sheila Malovany-Chevallier (New York: Vintage, 2009), 145.

6. Ibid., 146.

7. Footage of Wilding Davison's death is available on numerous YouTube sites. Of particular interest are the original 1913 British Pathé documentary of the incident and Clare Balding's 2013 documentary reconstruction of Wilding Davison's actions and her probable intentions. See "Emily Davison (Suffragette) Killed by King's Horse at Derby (1913)," British Pathé, https://www.youtube.com/watch?v=wVrlLKAR1S0; "Clare Balding's Secrets of a Suffragette / Epsom Derby Festival," Channel 4 Racing, https://www.youtube.com/watch?v=-W_URTWjgR0.

8. See Gavron, "Making of *Suffragette*," 987–88.

9. "War on Windows. Suffragette Raid on West End Shops," *Daily Graphic*, March 2, 1912. Article reproduced in Midge Mackenzie, *Shoulder to Shoulder: A Documentary* (Harmondsworth: Penguin, 1975), 187.

10. See Mackenzie, *Shoulder to Shoulder*, 162–68.

11. Linda Gordon, review of *Suffragette*, directed by Sarah Gavron, *Public Books*, November 10, 2015, http://www.publicbooks.org/artmedia/suffragettes-take-hollywood.

12. Ibid. I have taken the liberty of silently correcting a typographical error here. Gordon accidentally writes "Davidson" with a second *d*.

13. Mackenzie, *Shoulder to Shoulder*, 306–32.

14. E. Sylvia Pankhurst, *The Suffragette Movement: An Intimate Account of Persons and Ideals* (London: Longmans, Green and Co., 1931), 517.

15. Ibid.

16. Ibid., 519.

17. Joanne Laurier, review of *Suffragette*, directed by Sarah Gavron, *World Socialist Web Site*, November 28, 2015, https://www.wsws.org/en/articles/2015/11/28/suff-n28.html.

18. Ibid.

19. Ibid.

20. Ibid.

21. Beauvoir, *Second Sex*, 28.

22. Kimberle Crenshaw, "Demarginalizing the Intersection of Race and Sex: A Black Feminist Critique of Antidiscrimination Doctrine, Feminist Theory and Antiracist Politics," *University of Chicago Legal Forum* 140 (1989): 139–67.

23. Žižek, *Year of Dreaming Dangerously*, 33.

24. Paul Thompson, *The Edwardians: The Remaking of British Society*, second ed. (New York: Routledge, 1992), 171.

25. Žižek, *Year of Dreaming Dangerously*, 34.

26. Gavron describes the transformation of the old print factory into a working laundry facility in the feature commentary on the *Suffragette* DVD.

27. Michel Foucault, *Discipline and Punish: The Birth of the Prison*, trans. Alan Sheridan (New York: Vintage, 1979), 205.

28. Ibid., 200–01. For an interesting commentary on the relation between Foucault's writings on the Panopticon and Marx's writings on the birth of the modern factory, see David Harvey, *A Companion to Marx's "Capital"* (London: Verso, 2010), 148–49.

29. Chris Harman, *Zombie Capitalism: Global Crisis and the Relevance of Marx* (Chicago: Haymarket Books, 2010), 333.

30. Nina Power, *One-Dimensional Woman* (Winchester, UK: Zero Books, 2009), 20.

31. Saskia Sassen, *Globalization and Its Discontents: Essays on the New Mobility of People and Money* (New York: New Press, 1998), 111.

32. Ibid., 111–31.

33. "Trade Union Manual on Export Processing Zones," International Labour Organization, 2014, http://www.ilo.org/wcmsp5/groups/public/---ed_dialogue/---actrav/documents/publication/wcms_324632.pdf.

34. Naomi Klein, *No Logo*, tenth anniversary ed. (Toronto: Vintage Canada, 2009), 205.

35. For startling statistics on a handful of representative EPZs,

see Table 9.3 in ibid., 474.

36. Ibid., 327–29.

37. See Table 9.3 in ibid., 474.

38. Ibid., 212–13.

39. Ibid., 212.

40. For an analysis of the construction of consent in the United States and Great Britain, see David Harvey, *A Brief History of Neoliberalism* (Oxford: Oxford University Press, 2005), 39–63. For a gripping account of how this transformation took place in Kansas—a former hotbed of socialism and currently one of the most right-wing states in the United States—see Thomas Frank, *What's the Matter with Kansas? How Conservatives Won the Heart of America* (New York: Henry Holt and Company, 2004).

41. By calling our era "class-blind" I do not mean to imply that people do not see themselves and others as belonging to a certain social class but, rather, that our époque tends to perceive social class (especially the working class, or what used to be called "the proletariat") as a marker of identity as opposed to a collective subjectivity.

42. See Ira W. Howerth, "The Social Question of Today," *American Journal of Sociology* 12, no. 2 (September 1906): 254–68.

43. Cited in Jacques Rancière, *Hatred of Democracy*, trans. Steve Corcoran (London: Verso, 2006), 60.

44. Jacques Rancière, *Dissensus: On Politics and Aesthetics*, trans. Steven Corcoran (London: Continuum, 2010), 69.

45. Jacques Rancière, *Disagreement: Politics and Philosophy*, trans. Julie Rose (Minneapolis: University of Minnesota Press, 1999), 89.

46. Jacques Rancière, *On the Shores of Politics*, trans. Liz Heron (London: Verso, 2007), 45–52.

47. Ibid., 47.

48. Cited in Pankhurst, *Suffragette Movement*, 372.

Chapter 4 The Insurrection to Come: *Django Unchained*

1. Quentin Tarantino, interview by Henry Louis Gates Jr., part 2, *The Root*, December 24, 2012, http://www.theroot.com/ articles/history/2012/12/the_nword_in_django_unchained_ tarantinos_explanation/.
2. Quentin Tarantino, interview by Henry Louis Gates Jr., part 3, *The Root*, December 25, 2012, http://www.theroot.com/ articles/history/2012/12/django_unchained_and_the_white_ savior_what_tarantino_says/.
3. Jameson, *Political Unconscious*, 98.
4. Ibid., 99.
5. Tavis Smiley and Cornel West, *The Rich and the Rest of Us: A Poverty Manifesto* (New York: Smiley Books, 2012), 153.
6. Michael K. Johnson, "The D Is Silent: *Django Unchained* and the African American West," *Safundi* 16, no. 3 (2015): 257.
7. Johannes Fehrle, "'And I Would Call It "a Southern"': Renewing/Obscuring the Blaxploitation Western," *Safundi* 16, no. 3 (2015): 293; Fehrle's citation is from Richard Alleva, "Raw Spaghetti," *Commonweal*, March 13, 2013, 16.
8. Anne Thompson, "Tarantino's Next Movie is Black Western *Django Unchained* Confirmed and Updated," *Indiewire*, April 30, 2011, http://blogs.indiewire.com/thompsononhollywood/ tarantino_find_a_title_django_unchained.
9. Fehrle, "And I Would Call It 'a Southern,'" 294.
10. Adilifu Nama, *Race on the QT: Blackness in the Films of Quentin Tarantino* (Austin: University of Texas Press, 2015), 105.
11. Neil Campbell, "'Dollar in the Teeth': Upsetting the Post-Western after Leone or Worlding the Western," *Safundi* 16, no. 3 (2015): 272.
12. Christopher Frayling, *Spaghetti Westerns: Cowboys and Europeans From Karl May to Sergio Leone* (London: Routledge & Kegan Paul, 1981), 135; cited in Campbell, "Dollar in the Teeth," 272.
13. Jameson, *Political Unconscious*, 99.

14. Jameson's deservedly famous critique of pastiche in his seminal "Postmodernism" essay leaves little doubt that he would find Tarantino's aesthetic lacking in punch: "Pastiche is, like parody, the imitation of a peculiar or unique, idiosyncratic style, the wearing of a linguistic mask, speech in a dead language. But it is a neutral practice of such mimicry, without any of parody's ulterior motives, amputated of the satiric impulse, devoid of laughter and of any conviction that alongside the abnormal tongue you have momentarily borrowed, some healthy linguistic normality still exists. Pastiche is thus blank parody, a statue with blind eyeballs." Jameson, *Postmodernism*, 17.

15. Fredric Jameson, *The Cultural Turn: Selected Writings on the Postmodern, 1983–1998* (London: Verso, 2009), 74.

16. Ibid., 75.

17. Louis Hjelmslev, *Prolegomena to a Theory of Language*, trans. Francis J. Whitfield (Madison: University of Wisconsin Press, 1963), 118–19.

18. For a nice commentary on the costumes in *Django Unchained*, see Marine Hanel, "From Sketch to Still: The Spaghetti-Western Wit of Sharen Davis's *Django Unchained* Costumes," *Vanity Fair*, January 4, 2013, http://www.vanityfair.com/hollywood/2013/01/django-unchained-costume-design-oscar-nomination.

19. Margaret Ozierski, "Franco-faux-ne: Django's Jive," in *Quentin Tarantino's "Django Unchained": The Continuation of Metacinema*, ed. Oliver C. Speck (London: Bloomsbury, 2014), 43.

20. Ibid., 44.

21. Nama, *Race on the QT*, 108.

22. Ibid., 118.

23. David Roediger, *Seizing Freedom: Slave Emancipation and Liberty for All* (London: Verso, 2014), 105.

24. See ibid., 97.

25. See for example Judith Butler, *Gender Trouble: Feminism and the Subversion of Identity* (New York: Routledge, 1990), 24–25; Judith Butler, *Bodies that Matter: On the Discursive Limits of "Sex"* (New York: Routledge, 1993), 1–16.

26. Agamben, *Homo Sacer*, 52–54.

27. Nama, *Race on the QT*, 117.

28. Heather Ashley Hayes and Gilbert G. Rodman, "Thirteen Ways of Looking at a Black Film: What Does It Mean to Be a Black Film in Twenty-First Century America?" in *Quentin Tarantino's "Django Unchained": The Continuation of Metacinema*, ed. Oliver C. Speck (London: Bloomsbury, 2014), 189–90. The essay also appears in article form under the title "*Django Unchained*: Thirteen Ways of Looking at a Black Film" in *Jump Cut* 56 (Winter 2014–15), https://www.ejumpcut.org/archive/jc56.2014-2015/rodman-django/index.html.

29. Tarantino, interview by Gates, part 2.

30. Keeanga-Yamahtta Taylor, "Race, Class and Marxism," *The Socialist Worker*, January 4, 2011, http://socialistworker.org/2011/01/04/race-class-and-marxism.

31. Marx, *Capital*, vol. 1, 329.

32. William Brown, "Value and Violence in *Django Unchained*," in *Quentin Tarantino's "Django Unchained": The Continuation of Metacinema*, ed. Oliver C. Speck (London: Bloomsbury, 2014), 167.

33. Karl Marx, *On America and the Civil War*, vol. 2 of *The Karl Marx Library*, ed. and trans. Saul K. Padover (New York: McGraw-Hill, 1972), 36. Cited in a different translation in Brown, "Value and Violence," 166.

34. Marx, *On America and the Civil War*, 36.

35. Salome Lee, "Until We Are All Abolitionists: Marx on Slavery, Race, and Class," *U.S. Marxist-Humanists*, October 22, 2011, http://www.internationalmarxisthumanist.org/articles/abolitionists-marx-slavery-race-class-salome-lee.

36. Marx, *Capital*, vol. 1, 345.

37. Harvey, *Companion to Marx's "Capital,"* 127.

38. Marx, *Capital*, vol. 1, 345.

39. Marx, *On America and the Civil War*, 36.

40. Graeber, *Debt*, 120.

41. Ibid., 352. I have taken the liberty of silently correcting a typo in Graeber's sentence. The author accidently writes the second "you've" as "you're."

42. Friedrich Engels, *The Condition of the Working Class in England* (London: Penguin, 2009), 119; Marx, *Capital*, vol. 1, 781–94.

43. Marx, *Capital*, vol. 1, 798. Italics in original.

44. Ibid., 799.

45. Jameson, *Representing Capital*, 71.

46. Ibid., 9; Ernest Mandel, introduction to *Capital*, by Karl Marx (London: Penguin, 1976), 82.

47. Marx and Engels, *Communist Manifesto*, 10.

48. Ibid., 11.

49. Ibid., 13.

50. Ibid., 14.

51. Chris Hedges, *Wages of Rebellion: The Moral Imperative of Revolt* (Toronto: Knopf Canada, 2015), 2.

52. Cited in ibid., 3.

53. Ibid., 4.

54. Harvey, *Seventeen Contradictions*, 288.

55. Homi K. Bhabha, foreword to *The Wretched of the Earth*, by Frantz Fanon (New York: Grove Press, 2004), xiii.

56. Ibid., xxvii.

57. Fanon, *Wretched of the Earth*, 5.

58. Poverty Fact Sheet, *The State of Working America*, http://stateofworkingamerica.org/fact-sheets/poverty/, accessed July 19, 2016.

59. Cited in Dan Baum, "Legalize It All: How to Win the War on Drugs," *Harper's Magazine*, April 2016, http://harpers.org/archive/2016/04/legalize-it-all/.

60. Michelle Alexander, *The New Jim Crow: Mass Incarceration in the Age of Colorblindness* (New York: New Press, 2010), 6.
61. Madonna Gauding, "U.S. Companies Make a Killing off Prison Labor," *Occasional Planet,* December 1, 2015, http://www.occasionalplanet.org/2015/12/01/u-s-companies-make-a-killing-off-prison-slave-labor/.
62. See Rick Perlstein, "Exclusive: Lee Atwater's Infamous 1981 Interview on the Southern Strategy," *The Nation*, November 13, 2012, https://www.thenation.com/article/exclusive-lee-atwaters-infamous-1981-interview-southern-strategy/.
63. Fanon, *Wretched of the Earth*, 6.

Chapter 5 Negations of the Negation: *Elysium* and *Snowpiercer*

1. Slavoj Žižek, *Trouble in Paradise: From the End of History to the End of Capitalism* (London: Allen Lane, 2014), 61–62.
2. Ibid., 62.
3. Peter Sloterdijk, *In the World Interior of Capital*, trans. Wieland Hoban (Cambridge: Polity, 2013), 194–95.
4. Ibid., 193–94.
5. Ibid., 196.
6. Ibid., 171.
7. See Mark Salisbury, *Elysium: The Art of the Film*, foreword by Neill Blomkamp (London: Titan, 2013), 18–23, 116–29.
8. Neill Blomkamp cited in ibid., 20.
9. Mike Davis, *City of Quartz: Excavating the Future in Los Angeles* (London: Verso, 2006), 171.
10. Salisbury, *Elysium*, 116.
11. Phil Ivey cited in ibid., 127.
12. Saskia Sassen, "Urban Gating—One Instance of a Larger Development?" in *Gated Communities: Social Sustainability in Contemporary and Historical Gated Developments*, ed. Samer Bagaeen and Ola Uduku (London: Earthscan, 2010), xi.
13. Ibid., xi–xii.
14. It is to this "nation" that the editors unironically dedicate

the volume. *Beyond Gated Communities*, ed. Samer Bagaeen and Ola Uduku (London: Earthscan, 2015), xxi.

15. Mike Davis, *Planet of Slums* (London: Verso, 2006), 19.
16. Ivey cited in Salisbury, *Elysium*, 16.
17. Blomkamp cited ibid., 14.
18. Davis, *City of Quartz*, 18; Davis, *Planet of Slums*, 36.
19. Davis, *City of Quartz*, 227.
20. Fredric Jameson, *Archaeologies of the Future: The Desire Called Utopia and Other Science Fictions* (London: Verso, 2007), 345.
21. See Milo Sweedler, "Class Warfare in the *RoboCop* Films," *Jump Cut: A Review of Contemporary Media* 56 (Winter 2014–15), https://www.ejumpcut.org/archive/jc56.2014-2015/Swe edlerRobocop/index.html.
22. Harvey, *Seventeen Contradictions*, 103.
23. Ibid., 108.
24. Gillian B. White, "Are Factories in Bangladesh Any Safer Now?" *Atlantic*, December 17, 2015, https://www. theatlantic.com/business/archive/2015/12/bangladesh-factory-workers/421005/.
25. Joel Bakan, *The Corporation* (London: Constable, 2004), 35.
26. The law of falling profits is laid out most fully in Marx, *Capital*, vol. 3, 317–38. For cogent analyses of the law, see David Harvey, *The Limits to Capital*, new and fully updated ed. (London: Verso, 2006), 176–89; Harman, *Zombie Capitalism*, 68–81.
27. Marx, *Capital*, vol. 3, 318.
28. Harvey, *Limits to Capital*, 183.
29. Karl Marx, *Grundrisse*, trans. Martin Nicolaus (London: Penguin, 1993), 748.
30. See Marx, *Capital*, vol. 3, 339–48.
31. For nice overviews of this controversy, see Harvey, *Limits to Capital*, 176–89; Harman, *Zombie Capitalism*, 68–81.
32. Marx, *Capital*, vol. 1, 929.
33. Ibid.

34. Ibid.
35. Ibid., 930 n. 2.
36. Harvey, *Limits to Capital*, 188.
37. Cited in Slavoj Žižek, "Lenin's Choice," in V.I. Lenin, *Revolution at the Gates*, ed. Slavoj Žižek (London: Verso, 2002), 292–93.
38. Fredric Jameson, *Valences of the Dialectic* (London: Verso, 2010), 571, 580.
39. Žižek, *Trouble in Paradise*, 22.
40. Davis, *Planet of Slums*, 176.
41. Naomi Klein, *This Changes Everything: Capitalism vs. the Climate* (Toronto: Knopf Canada, 2014), 21.
42. Ibid., 258.
43. Cited in ibid., 270.
44. Louis Althusser, *Lenin and Philosophy and Other Essays*, trans. Ben Brewster (New York: Monthly Review Press, 1971), 139.
45. Fisher, *Capitalist Realism*, 8.
46. Slavoj Žižek, *The Universal Exception* (London: Continuum, 2006), 104.
47. Georg Lukács, *History and Class Consciousness: Studies in Marxist Dialectics*, trans. Rodney Livingstone (Cambridge, MA: MIT Press, 1971), 43.
48. Žižek, *Universal Exception*, 106.
49. Karl Marx, *The Eighteenth Brumaire of Louis Bonaparte* (New York: International Publishers, 1963), 75.
50. Mikhail Bakunin, *Bakunin on Anarchy*, ed., trans., and with an introduction by Sam Dolgoff (New York: Vintage, 1971), 294.
51. Peter Marshall, *Demanding the Impossible: A History of Anarchism* (London: Harper Perennial, 2008), 304.
52. Saul Newman, *The Politics of Postanarchism* (Edinburgh: Edinburgh University Press, 2011), 86.
53. Marx and Engels, *Communist Manifesto*, 39.
54. Harman, *Zombie Capitalism*, 336.

55. Karl Marx and Friedrich Engels, *Manifesto of the Communist Party* (Chicago: Charles H. Kerr, 1888), 27.
56. Marx, *Capital*, vol. 1, 797.
57. Jameson, *Valences*, 577.
58. Bakunin cited in Marshall, *Demanding the Impossible*, 295.
59. Cited in ibid., 306.

Bibliography

Agamben, Giorgio. *Homo Sacer: Sovereign Power and Bare Life.* Trans. Daniel Heller-Roazen. Stanford: Stanford University Press, 1998.

Alexander, Michelle. *The New Jim Crow: Mass Incarceration in the Age of Colorblindness.* New York: New Press, 2010.

Althusser, Louis. *Lenin and Philosophy and Other Essays.* Trans. Ben Brewster. New York: Monthly Review Press, 1971.

Badiou, Alain. *The Rebirth of History: Times of Riots and Uprisings.* Trans. Gregory Elliott. London: Verso, 2012.

Bagaeen, Samer, and Ola Uduku, eds. *Beyond Gated Communities.* London: Earthscan, 2015.

Bakan, Joel. *The Corporation.* London: Constable, 2004.

Bakunin, Mikhail. *Bakunin on Anarchy.* Ed., trans., and with an introduction by Sam Dolgoff. New York: Vintage, 1971.

Beaumont, Matthew. "Imagining the End Times: Ideology, the Contemporary Disaster Movie, *Contagion.*" In *Žižek and Media Studies: A Reader,* ed. Matthew Flisfeder and Louis-Paul Willis, 79-89. New York: Palgrave Macmillan, 2014.

Beauvoir, Simone de. *The Second Sex.* Trans. Constance Borde and Sheila Malovany-Chevallier. New York: Vintage, 2009.

Benjamin, Walter. *Selected Writings.* Vol. 1. Ed. Marcus Bullock and Michael W. Jennings. Cambridge, MA: Harvard University Press, 2004.

Benson-Allott, Caetlin. "The Minor Cronenberg." *New Review of Film and Television Studies* 15, no. 2 (2017): 152–61.

Bhabha, Homi K. Foreword to *The Wretched of the Earth,* by Frantz Fanon. New York: Grove Press, 2004.

Boyle, Kirk. "Three Ways of Looking at a Neoliberalist: Mobile Global Traffic in *Cosmopolis* and *Nightcrawler.*" *Quarterly Review of Film and Video* 34, no. 6 (2017): 535–59.

Boyle, Kirk, and Daniel Mrozowski, eds. *The Great Recession in*

Fiction, Film, and Television: Twenty-First Century Bust Culture.
Lanham, MD: Rowman & Littlefield, 2013.

Brecht, Bertolt. *Brecht on Theatre.* Ed. and trans. John Willett.
New York: Hill and Wang, 1957.

Butler, Judith. *Bodies that Matter: On the Discursive Limits of "Sex."*
New York: Routledge, 1993.

—. "Critique, Coercion, and Sacred Life in Benjamin's 'Critique
of Violence.'" In *Political Theologies: Public Religions in a Post-
Secular World,* eds. Hent de Vries and Lawrence E. Sullivan,
201–19. Bronx, NY: Fordham University Press, 2006.

—. *Gender Trouble: Feminism and the Subversion of Identity.* New
York: Routledge, 1990.

Butler, Judith, Ernesto Laclau, and Slavoj Žižek. *Contingency,
Hegemony, Universality.* London: Verso, 2000.

Campbell, Neil. "'Dollar in the Teeth': Upsetting the Post-
Western after Leone or Worlding the Western." *Safundi* 16,
no. 3 (2015): 267–79.

Copeland, Rita, and Peter T. Struck, eds. *The Cambridge Companion
to Allegory.* Cambridge: Cambridge University Press, 2010.

Cosmopolis. Directed by David Cronenberg. 2012. Toronto:
Entertainment One, 2013. DVD.

Crenshaw, Kimberle. "Demarginalizing the Intersection of Race
and Sex: A Black Feminist Critique of Antidiscrimination
Doctrine, Feminist Theory and Antiracist Politics." *University
of Chicago Legal Forum* 140 (1989): 139–67.

Critchley, Simon. *The Faith of the Faithless: Experiments in Political
Theology.* London: Verso, 2012.

Dargis, Manohla. "This is How the End Begins." *New York Times,*
December 30, 2011. http://www.nytimes.com/2012/01/01/
movies/awardsseason/manohla-dargis-looks-at-the-over
ture-to-melancholia.html?_r=1.

Davis, Mike. *City of Quartz: Excavating the Future in Los Angeles.*
London: Verso, 2006.

—. *Planet of Slums.* London: Verso, 2006.

DeLillo, Don. *Cosmopolis*. New York: Scribner, 2003.

Derrida, Jacques. *Acts of Religion*. Ed. Gil Anidjar. New York: Routledge, 2002.

—. *Specters of Marx*. Trans. Peggy Kamuf. New York: Routledge, 1994.

Django Unchained. Directed by Quentin Tarantino. 2012. Montreal: Alliance, 2013. DVD.

Elysium. Directed by Neill Blomkamp. 2013. Culver City, CA: Sony, 2013. DVD.

Engels, Friedrich. *The Condition of the Working Class in England*. London: Penguin, 2009.

Fanon, Frantz. *The Wretched of the Earth*. Trans. Richard Philcox. New York: Grove Press, 2004.

Fehrle, Johannes. "'And I Would Call It "a Southern"': Renewing/ Obscuring the Blaxploitation Western." *Safundi* 16, no. 3 (2015): 291–306.

Figlerowicz, Marta. "Comedy of Abandon: Lars von Trier's *Melancholia*." *Film Quarterly* 65, no. 4 (2012): 21–26.

Fisher, Mark. *Capitalist Realism: Is There No Alternative?* Winchester, UK: Zero Books, 2009.

Fisk, John. *Understanding Popular Culture*. London: Routledge, 1989.

Foucault, Michel. *Discipline and Punish: The Birth of the Prison*. Trans. Alan Sheridan. New York: Vintage, 1979.

Frank, Thomas. *What's the Matter with Kansas? How Conservatives Won the Heart of America*. New York: Henry Holt and Company, 2004.

Fromm, Erich. *Marx's Concept of Man*. New York: Frederick Ungar, 1961.

Fukuyama, Francis. *The End of History and the Last Man*. New York: Free Press, 2006.

Gavron, Sarah. "The Making of the Feature Film *Suffragette*." *Women's History Review* 24, no. 6 (2015): 985–95. http://dx.doi.org/10.1080/09612025.2015.1074007.

Gordon, Linda. Review of *Suffragette*, directed by Sarah Gavron. *Public Books*, November 10, 2015. http://www.publicbooks. org/artmedia/suffragettes-take-hollywood.

Graeber, David. *Debt: The First 5,000 Years*. Updated and expanded ed. Brooklyn: Melville House, 2014.

Harman, Chris. *Zombie Capitalism: Global Crisis and the Relevance of Marx*. Chicago: Haymarket, 2010.

Harvey, David. *A Brief History of Neoliberalism*. Oxford: Oxford University Press, 2005.

—. *A Companion to Marx's "Capital."* London: Verso, 2010.

—. *The Enigma of Capital and the Crises of Capitalism*. With a new afterword. Oxford: Oxford University Press, 2011.

—. *The Limits to Capital*. New and fully updated ed. London: Verso, 2006.

—. *Seventeen Contradictions and the End of Capitalism*. Oxford: Oxford University Press, 2014.

Hayes, Heather Ashley, and Gilbert G. Rodman. "*Django Unchained*: Thirteen Ways of Looking at a Black Film." In *Jump Cut* 56 (Winter 2014–15). https://www.ejumpcut.org/archive/ jc56.2014-2015/rodman-django/index.html.

Hedges, Chris. *Wages of Rebellion: The Moral Imperative of Revolt*. Toronto: Knopf Canada, 2015.

Jameson, Fredric. *Archaeologies of the Future: The Desire Called Utopia and Other Science Fictions*. London: Verso, 2007.

—. *Brecht and Method*. London: Verso, 1999.

—. "Cognitive Mapping." In *Marxism and the Interpretation of Culture*. Ed. Cary Nelson and Lawrence Grossberg, 347–60. Champaign: University of Illinois Press, 1988.

—. "Future City." *New Left Review* 21 (May–June 2003), 65–79.

—. *The Geopolitical Aesthetic: Cinema and Space in the World System*. Bloomington: Indiana University Press, 1992.

—. *The Political Unconscious: Narrative as a Socially Symbolic Act*. Ithaca: Cornell University Press, 1981.

—. *Postmodernism, .or, The Cultural Logic of Late Capitalism*.

Durham: Duke University Press, 1991.

—. *Representing Capital: A Reading of Volume One*. London: Verso, 2011.

—. *The Seeds of Time*. New York: Columbia University Press, 1994.

—. *Signatures of the Visible*. New York: Routledge, 1992.

—. *Valences of the Dialectic*. London: Verso, 2010.

Johnson, Michael K. "The D Is Silent: *Django Unchained* and the African American West." *Safundi* 16, no. 3 (2015): 256–66.

Klein, Naomi. *No Logo*. Tenth anniversary ed. Toronto: Vintage Canada, 2009.

—. *This Changes Everything: Capitalism vs. the Climate*. Toronto: Knopf Canada, 2014.

Kojève, Alexandre. *Introduction to the Reading of Hegel: Lectures on the Phenomenology of Spirit*. Assembled by Raymond Queneau. Ed. Alan Bloom. Trans. James H. Nichols, Jr. Ithaca: Cornell University Press, 1980.

Kracauer, Siegfried. *From Caligari to Hitler: A Psychological History of the German Film*. Revised and expanded ed. Ed. and introduced by Leonardo Quaresima. Princeton: Princeton University Press, 2004.

—. *The Mass Ornament: Weimar Essays*. Ed. and trans. Thomas Y. Levin. Cambridge, MA: Harvard University Press, 1995.

Laurier, Joanne. Review of *Suffragette*, directed by Sarah Gavron. *World Socialist Web Site*, November 28, 2015. https://www. wsws.org/en/articles/2015/11/28/suff-n28.html.

Lee, Salome. "Until We Are All Abolitionists: Marx on Slavery, Race, and Class." *U.S. Marxist-Humanists*, October 22, 2011. http://www.internationalmarxisthumanist.org/articles/ abolitionists-marx-slavery-race-class-salome-lee.

Liddington, Jill. *Rebel Girls: Their Fight for the Vote*. London: Virago, 2006.

Lukács, Georg. *History and Class Consciousness: Studies in Marxist Dialectics*. Trans. Rodney Livingstone. Cambridge, MA: MIT Press, 1971.

Mackenzie, Midge. *Shoulder to Shoulder: A Documentary.* Harmondsworth: Penguin, 1975.

Marshall, Peter. *Demanding the Impossible: A History of Anarchism.* London: Harper Perennial, 2008.

Marx, Karl. *Capital.* Vol. 1. Trans. Ben Fowkes. London: Penguin, 1976.

—. *Capital.* Vol. 3. Trans. David Fernbach. London: Penguin, 1981.

—. *A Contribution to the Critique of Political Economy.* Trans. N.I. Stone. New York: International Publishers, 1970.

—. "Economic and Philosophical Manuscripts." Trans. T.B. Bottomore. In Erich Fromm, *Marx's Concept of Man*, 93–109. New York: Frederick Ungar, 1961.

—. *The Eighteenth Brumaire of Louis Bonaparte.* New York: International Publishers, 1963.

—. *Grundrisse.* Trans. Martin Nicolaus. London: Penguin, 1993.

—. *On America and the Civil War.* Vol. 2 of *The Karl Marx Library.* Ed. and trans. Saul K. Padover. New York: McGraw-Hill, 1972.

Marx, Karl, and Friedrich Engels. *The Communist Manifesto.* Oxford: Oxford University Press, 1998.

Nama, Adilifu. *Race on the QT: Blackness and the Films of Quentin Tarantino.* Austin: University of Texas Press, 2015.

Newman, Saul. *The Politics of Postanarchism.* Edinburgh: Edinburgh University Press, 2011.

Pankhurst, E. Sylvia. *The Suffragette Movement: An Intimate Account of Persons and Ideals.* London: Longmans, Green and Co., 1931.

Paxton, Robert O. *Anatomy of Fascism.* New York: Vintage, 2004.

Piketty, Thomas. *Capital in the Twenty-First Century.* Trans. Arthur Goldhammer. Cambridge, MA: Harvard University Press, 2014.

Power, Nina. *One-Dimensional Woman.* Winchester, UK: Zero Books, 2009.

Rancière, Jacques. *Disagreement: Politics and Philosophy*. Trans. Julie Rose. Minneapolis: University of Minnesota Press, 1999.

—. *Dissensus: On Politics and Aesthetics*. Trans. Steven Corcoran. London: Continuum, 2010.

—. *Hatred of Democracy*. Trans. Steve Corcoran. London: Verso, 2006.

—. *On the Shores of Politics*. Trans. Liz Heron. London: Verso, 2007.

Roediger, David. *Seizing Freedom: Slave Emancipation and Liberty for All*. London: Verso, 2014.

Salisbury, Mark. *Elysium: The Art of the Film*. Foreword by Neill Blomkamp. London: Titan, 2013.

Sartre, Jean-Paul. *Being and Nothingness*. Trans. Hazel E. Barnes. New York: Washington Square Press, 1956.

Sassen, Saskia. *Globalization and Its Discontents: Essays on the New Mobility of People and Money*. New York: New Press, 1998.

—. "Urban Gating—One Instance of a Larger Development?" In *Gated Communities: Social Sustainability in Contemporary and Historical Gated Developments*, ed. Samer Bagaeen and Ola Uduku, xi–xii. London: Earthscan, 2010.

Shaviro, Steven. "*Melancholia*, or, the Romantic Anti-Sublime." *Sequence* 1, no. 1 (2012). http://reframe.sussex.ac.uk/sequence1/1-1-melancholia-or-the-romantic-anti-sublime.

Slaymaker, James. Review of *Cosmopolis*, directed by David Cronenberg. *Film International* 12, no. 4 (December 2014): 127–31.

Sloterdijk, Peter. *In the World Interior of Capital*. Trans. Wieland Hoban. Cambridge: Polity, 2013.

Smiley, Tavis, and Cornel West. *The Rich and the Rest of Us: A Poverty Manifesto*. New York: Smiley Books, 2012.

Snowpiercer. Directed by Bong Joon-ho. 2013. Toronto: Entertainment One, 2014. DVD.

Speck, Oliver C., ed. *Quentin Tarantino's "Django Unchained": The Continuation of Metacinema*. London: Bloomsbury, 2014.

Suffragette. Directed by Sarah Gavron. 2015. Universal City, CA: Universal, 2016. DVD.

Sweedler, Milo. "Class Warfare in the *RoboCop* Films." *Jump Cut: A Review of Contemporary Media* 56 (Winter 2014–15). https://www.ejumpcut.org/archive/jc56.2014–2015/Swee dlerRobocop/index.html.

—. *Rumble and Crash: Crises of Capitalism in Contemporary Film*. Horizons of Cinema. Albany: SUNY Press, 2019.

Tarantino, Quentin. Interview by Henry Louis Gates Jr. 3 parts. *The Root*, December 23, 24, and 25, 2012. http://www.theroot. com/articles/history/2012/12/django_unchained_trilogy_ and_more_tarantino_talks_to_gates/.

Taubin, Amy. Review of *Cosmopolis*, directed by David Cronenberg. *Artforum* 51, no. 1 (September 2012): 468–71.

Taylor, Keeanga-Yamahtta. "Race, Class and Marxism." *The Socialist Worker*, January 4, 2011. http://socialistworker. org/2011/01/04/race-class-and-marxism.

Thompson, Paul. *The Edwardians: The Remaking of British Society*. Second ed. New York: Routledge, 1992.

Toscano, Alberto, and Jeff Kinkle. *Cartographies of the Absolute*. Winchester, UK: Zero Books, 2015.

Truffaut, François. *Hitchcock*. Revised ed. New York: Simon & Schuster, 1984.

White, Micah. *The End of Protest: A New Playbook for Revolution*. Toronto: Knopf Canada, 2016.

Žižek, Slavoj. *First as Tragedy, Then as Farce*. London: Verso, 2009.

—. *In Defense of Lost Causes*. London: Verso, 2008.

—. "Lenin's Choice." In V.I. Lenin, *Revolution at the Gates*, ed. Slavoj Žižek, 167–336. London: Verso, 2002.

—. "Robespierre, or the Divine Violence of Terror." In Žižek Presents Robespierre: Virtue and Terror, ed. Jean Ducange, vii–xxxix. London: Verso, 2007.

—. *Trouble in Paradise: From the End of History to the End of Capitalism*. London: Allen Lane, 2014.

—. *The Universal Exception*. London: Continuum, 2006.

—. *Violence: Six Sideways Reflections*. New York: Picador, 2008.

—. *The Year of Dreaming Dangerously*. London: Verso, 2012.

CULTURE, SOCIETY & POLITICS

Contemporary culture has eliminated the concept and public figure of the intellectual. A cretinous anti-intellectualism presides, cheer-led by hacks in the pay of multinational corporations who reassure their bored readers that there is no need to rouse themselves from their stupor. Zer0 Books knows that another kind of discourse – intellectual without being academic, popular without being populist – is not only possible: it is already flourishing. Zer0 is convinced that in the unthinking, blandly consensual culture in which we live, critical and engaged theoretical reflection is more important than ever before.
If you have enjoyed this book, why not tell other readers by posting a review on your preferred book site.
Recent bestsellers from Zero Books are:

In the Dust of This Planet
Horror of Philosophy vol. 1
Eugene Thacker
In the first of a series of three books on the Horror of Philosophy, *In the Dust of This Planet* offers the genre of horror as a way of thinking about the unthinkable.
Paperback: 978-1-84694-676-9 ebook: 978-1-78099-010-1

Capitalist Realism
Is There no Alternative?
Mark Fisher
An analysis of the ways in which capitalism has presented itself as the only realistic political-economic system.
Paperback: 978-1-84694-317-1 ebook: 978-1-78099-734-6

Rebel Rebel
Chris O'Leary
David Bowie: every single song. Everything you want to know, everything you didn't know.
Paperback: 978-1-78099-244-0 ebook: 978-1-78099-713-1

Cartographies of the Absolute
Alberto Toscano, Jeff Kinkle
An aesthetics of the economy for the twenty-first century.
Paperback: 978-1-78099-275-4 ebook: 978-1-78279-973-3

Malign Velocities
Accelerationism and Capitalism
Benjamin Noys
Long listed for the Bread and Roses Prize 2015, *Malign Velocities* argues against the need for speed, tracking acceleration as the symptom of the ongoing crises of capitalism.
Paperback: 978-1-78279-300-7 ebook: 978-1-78279-299-4

Meat Market
Female Flesh under Capitalism
Laurie Penny
A feminist dissection of women's bodies as the fleshy fulcrum of capitalist cannibalism, whereby women are both consumers and consumed.
Paperback: 978-1-84694-521-2 ebook: 978-1-84694-782-7

Poor but Sexy
Culture Clashes in Europe East and West
Agata Pyzik
How the East stayed East and the West stayed West.
Paperback: 978-1-78099-394-2 ebook: 978-1-78099-395-9

Romeo and Juliet in Palestine
Teaching Under Occupation
Tom Sperlinger
Life in the West Bank, the nature of pedagogy and the role of a
university under occupation.
Paperback: 978-1-78279-637-4 ebook: 978-1-78279-636-7

Sweetening the Pill
or How We Got Hooked on Hormonal Birth Control
Holly Grigg-Spall
Has contraception liberated or oppressed women? *Sweetening
the Pill* breaks the silence on the dark side of hormonal
contraception.
Paperback: 978-1-78099-607-3 ebook: 978-1-78099-608-0

Why Are We The Good Guys?
Reclaiming your Mind from the Delusions of Propaganda
David Cromwell
A provocative challenge to the standard ideology that Western
power is a benevolent force in the world.
Paperback: 978-1-78099-365-2 ebook: 978-1-78099-366-9

Readers of ebooks can buy or view any of these bestsellers by
clicking on the live link in the title. Most titles are published
in paperback and as an ebook. Paperbacks are available in
traditional bookshops. Both print and ebook formats are available
online.
Find more titles and sign up to our readers' newsletter
at http://www.johnhuntpublishing.com/culture-and-politics
Follow us on Facebook
at https://www.facebook.com/ZeroBooks
and Twitter at https://twitter.com/Zer0Books